Creations in Miniature

101 Tiny Treasures
to Stitch
&
Craft

Published by

**krause
publications**

700 East State Street, Iola, WI 54990-0001

Please call or write for our free catalog of sewing and craft publications. Our toll-free number to place an order or obtain a free catalog is 800-258-0929 or please use our regular business telephone 715-445-2214 for editorial comment and further information.

Library of Congress Catalog Number: 98-84107
ISBN: 0-87341-574-4
Printed in the United States of America

Creations *in* Miniature

Author/Editor
Eleanor Levie

Art Director
Lisa J. F. Palmer

Photographers
George Ross

Tracey Hanover

Technical Illustrator
Eric Merrill

Designers
Kathleen George

Judi Kauffman

Michele Maks Thompson

Linda Driscoll

Barbara E. Swanson

Judy Barker

Jane "Shana" Blum

Kathryn Severns

Bonita Salamanca

Penny Kimball

Packaging: **Eleanor Levie/Craft Services**

Table of Contents

Adornments 8

Keepsakes 28

Traditions 54

$\mathcal{V}$IGNETTES   84

$\mathcal{B}$ASICS

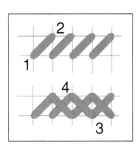

Introduction

The facination for artistic little objects is a universal one. Just as men never outgrow model railroads, women seem to be forever drawn to miniature paintings and lockets, dolls and dollhouses. My enthusiasm for small, antique quilts led to my first book, *Great Little Quilts,* and my favorite entries in that book are the most diminutive doll quilts. I just can't resist a beautifully crafted item that fits in the palm of my hand. Although my husband, son and I live in a big house where little accessories look fussy or lost, I simply group my small pieces together, such as my collection of little boxes. I proudly display those on a table in our sunroom. I take great pleasure in admiring these boxes, some handmade, some gifts, some souvenirs from around the world. While I don't have a dollhouse—yet, I've been in the dreaming and planning stages for years. Because I don't have a little girl, I'm putting off the self-indul-

gent luxury of building and furnishing a dollhouse that's just for me. I know I'm not alone in my desire to have one, though. Is it any surprise that the most popular attractions at Windsor Castle and museums like the Cooper-Hewitt in New York are the dollhouses? It must be so: Beautifully made, small-scale objects have a strong and long-abiding appeal to the heart.

The designs in this book draw on the lush and detailed style of the Victorian era, when craftsmanship and artistry rebelled against the coldness of the Machine Age. Then and now, miniatures provide the perfect refuge from an unsentimental world. They take the rough edges off reality. They allow us to preserve the past by recreating it, and they give us control over a tiny world of our own making. One miniature painter I know says she feels almost like a god

when she peers down at her little creations. And as gifts, miniature needlework and crafts objects are unparalleled. One can never be afraid to give a tiny, handmade thing to any man or woman. Everyone knows that good things come in small packages, and everyone is certain to have the room for such a gift.

This book started out as a collection of work by my favorite designers who usually work in small scale. I loved working closely with them to create a varied but cohesive collection of projects, infused with an overall feeling of nostalgia. As it turns out, I was so inspired by the breadth of their imaginations, I could not resist adding my own handiwork. I am a true dilettante, dabbling in lots of different needlework and crafts techniques. While that makes me a Jackie of all trades, mistress of none, the time I spend stitching and crafting is always fascinating and fun—never tedious. In exploring a new area, it is easy and even inevitable to put a personal stamp on an old tradition. There are so many great products at craft stores and sewing stores to ease one's initiation into a new technique (like modeling compounds with a stone-like texture), or to rejuvenate an old one (like rayon and metallic threads for embroidery). Among the pages that follow, you will find techniques that have long enjoyed great popularity, such as cross stitch, knit and crochet, needlepoint and stenciling. There are also nostalgic crafts currently in enthusiastic revival, such as ribbon embroidery and beadwork. And there are several innovative methods here, like using metallic powders on modeling compounds, foundation piecing and free-motion stitchery on the sewing machine, dollhouse twig-furniture construction, and rubber stamping on shrink art plastic. The beautiful materials—inexpensive since you need so little—and the elegance of the end product disguise the simplicity of the techniques. Because the items are small, most of them can be made in just one evening. However, the amazement and wonderment of onlookers will be in indirect proportion to the size of the piece you made. In other words, the smaller the piece, the more abundant the compliments!

In presenting the projects in this book, I define the term miniature very loosely. While making assignments to the designers, I suggested four inches as a maximum for any one dimension. On the other hand, pieces designed to work in a standard dollhouse were usually scaled at one inch representing one foot. So, while the quilts are larger than four inches, they fit most standard-scale doll beds. Sometimes, a design was merely a miniaturized version of the real thing, such as the chimney used as a bookend, which is somewhat oversized for most dollhouses. We may have taken a bit of crea-

tive license with the jewelry (Adornments) and the home accessories (Keepsakes), such that each piece merely fits in the palm of one's hand. In a nutshell, everything seemed to conform with our subjective definition of a tiny treasure!

In any and all cases, these creations in miniature are works of hand and heart. I hope they inspire you to bring your own personal vision to the making of them, customizing colors and details to suit you or those for whom they're intended. Be sure to sign and date your handiwork in some inconspicuous place. These microcosmic delights are today's tokens of affection and craftsmanship— and tomorrow's precious heirlooms.

"The world of reality has its limits; the world of imagination is boundless. Not being able to enlarge the one, let us contract the other."
—Jean Rousseau, 18th century Swiss philosopher

"Attention to small things is the economy of virtue."
—Chinese proverb

"Every gift, though it be small, is in reality great if given with affection."
—Pindar, 522-443 B.C.

Chapter One

Adornments

The word "miniature" is derived from work done in minium, a red lead pigment used in manuscript lettering, or illumination. Later, "miniature" was applied to illustration and small-size portraiture used in manuscripts. Soon came miniature portraits in lockets, with a great deal of attention given to the decoration of the piece. Miniatures and jewelry have since shared many attributes. They are elite, petite, precious.

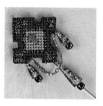 The personal accessories in this chapter are like little jewels. Elegant materials, such as silk ribbon, iridescent threads and glass beads are luxurious, but because you don't need much of them, they hardly put a crimp in your pocketbook. And, because the handwork covers such a small area, most of these designs can be fashioned in a mere hour or two.

Milady's Finery

The small scale of each of these elegant pieces guarantees that they will accent, not monopolize the wearer's style. Judi Kauffman's choker ornament and stick pin are like diminutive architecture. To accompany the stick pin, I fashioned four others from modeling compound and studded them with beads, brads, and ball chain. Inspired by Judi's sketches, I sewed the necklace purses, and

added swags and dangles of glass beads. Under the flap, the little pockets are just the right size to hold a key, a handkerchief, or a tube of lipstick. More glass beads from Mill Hill join with ribbon embroidery to lavishly embellish two romantic accents in Art Nouveau style. Depending on the finding that is affixed to the back of the perforated paper shapes, these might serve as barrettes, bolas, brooches or belt fasteners.

11

Adornments

Brooch the Subject

Small as it may be, one wonderful pin accenting a collar or securing a scarf will bring all eyes over to you, and show off your needleart skills. No need to tell admirers how simple it was to create. Above left, Judi Kauffman worked just a few embroidery stitches with Bucilla silk ribbons, added a few tiny beads and a bit of novelty threads, yet she achieved maximum effect. A rich fuchsia background brings

drama to the soft pastels. On a plane back from France and brimming with images of Cluny tapestries, Judi worked the petit-point floral of continental stitches, above right. Metallic threads, used sparingly, and a filigree frame in antique gold glint as they reflect the light. Dollhouse afficionados: Consider one of these designs for a pillow or cushion to scale, or framed as shown but mounted above diminutive furnishings.

From Head to Toe

These hair combs have their charms, and carry a message as well. I started with some lyrical script from my home computer, but a pertinent thought from a Chinese fortune cookie or any words reduced with a photocopier would work just as well. In a second set of combs, I combined clock parts from old wristwatches no longer operational with a winged angel charm, to gently admonish the viewer that time on earth is short and must be relished. A collage of buttons, baubles and ribbon roses softens the "pearls" of wisdom. Wrapping the crystal combs underneath are silk ribbons from Bucilla, which are also used, along with organza ribbons, in Judi Kauffman's shoe embellishments. While the ribbonwork shown here is done directly on the toes, one could just as easily fashion the rosebuds on separate little rectangles one can clip onto pumps and detach at will.

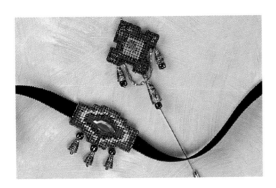

NEEDLEPOINT STICKPIN AND CHOKER

Dimensions of needlepoint areas only:
Stickpin, 1¼″ square; Choker, 2″ by 1″.

Materials & Tools

- Kreinik Medium Braid #16, 1 skein each color listed in the key
- Anchor 6-strand floss from Coats & Clark, 1 skein each color listed in the key
- Kreinik ¹⁄₁₆″ Metallic Ribbon: for both, Steel Gray #010HL; also for Choker, Curry #2122
- Mill Hill Beads: Midnight Rainbow Glass Pebble Beads #05086; also for Stickpin,
- Glass Seed Beads in Old Rose #00553, Gold #00557, and Petite Seed Beads in Gold #40557; also for Choker, Glass Seed Beads in Red Red #02013
- Beadworks beads: Japanese glass lampwork conical beads with foil inserts; for Stickpin, one C71, two A71; for Choker, three A71
- Beadworks findings: for Stickpin, AL 01 (gold) or 02 (silver); for Choker, necklace hooks N, P, Q, R, S, T or V
- Black sewing thread
- 14-count plastic canvas from Darice
- Aleene's Tacky Glue
- Scraps of Ultrasuede (or felt), for backing
- Tapestry and beading needles

Also for Choker:
- Aqua acrylic jewel #7372, from Westrim Crafts
- ½ yard black velvet ribbon, ³⁄₈″ wide

Directions

Stitching: Needlepoint on plastic canvas following the appropriate chart and key. Work the center of the Stickpin in long stitches, referring to the chart for length, direction, and color of these stitches. Work everything else in continental stitch, referring to the Needlepoint Know-How on the opposite page. Use all 6 strands of embroidery floss, or medium braid.

Shaping: Cut out the stitched shape, leaving one row of plastic beyond the stitches. Overcast the edges using ¹⁄₁₆″ metallic ribbon and a simple, diagonal stitch. For the best coverage, make 3 stitches at each outer corner.

Beadwork: Thread a beading needle with black thread and pull threads' ends even. Bring the needle through a few stitches on the back, emerging where beads are desired. Take 2 tiny backstitches to secure the thread. Thread on beads in the order as follows or as desired. Always end with a seed bead, and bring the needle back the same way. Wrap it around the thread at the beginning of the bead sequence and through a few stitches on the back of the needlepoint. Clip threads close to the surface where they emerge.

For the Stickpin, place an Old Rose seed bead, lampwork bead, pebble bead, and another Old Rose seed bead at each bottom corner, using the large lampwork bead at the center. Add a swag of gold beads between the bottom corners. Begin and end with a seed bead using 5 seed beads altogether and threading on 8 petite beads in between them. Optionally, stitch an Old Rose seed bead to the remaining corners of the needlepoint.

For the Choker, place the following sequence of beads at the bottom center and ½″ to either side, at the outer corners of the stepped row: red seed bead, pebble bead, lampwork bead, red seed bead. Additionally, glue an acrylic jewel horizontally across the center of the needlework area.

Finishing: Trace needlework pieces onto the backing material. Cut it out, ¹⁄₈″ smaller all around. Glue a stickpin finding down the center of the Stickpin needlepoint. Glue velvet ribbon across the center of the Choker needlepoint. Glue backings in place and allow them to dry. For the Choker, trim each velvet end ½″ larger than needed to fit. Turn ends ¼″ into wrong side twice, and stitch closure findings in place. ◊

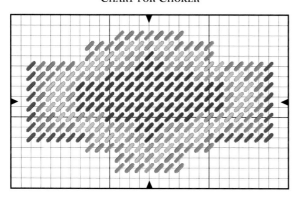

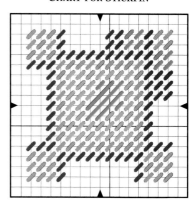

KEY

Anchor Six-Strand Floss

━ Red #46

━ Ecru #387

Kreinik #16 Medium Braid

━ Turquoise #029

━ Confetti #034

━ Red #003

KEY

Anchor Six-Strand Floss

━ Raspberry #89

━ Pale Olive #945

Kreinik #16 Medium Braid

━ Confetti #034

━ Turquoise #029

Needlepoint Know-How

To begin, leave a short, 1" tail on the back and work over it to secure it in place. To end, insert the needle under a few stitches on the back. Do not make knots. For the continental stitch, bring the needle up through the canvas where indicated on the detail by the number 1. Bring the needle down at 2, up at 3, and down at 4. Proceed with this diagonal pattern for each same-color symbol on the chart until you get to the end of the row. Turn work and chart upside down so that you can work even rows from right to left also. Finish working all symbols for the first color, then proceed to the second color and work all stitches for that color. Continue in this way until needlepoint is completed.

STICKPIN SCULPTURES

Dimensions: 2⅝" to 3¾"

Materials & Tools

- ❀ *Fimo Modeling Material from AMACO (hereafter referred to as "clay"), 1 package each Pink, Light Turquoise, Red*
- ❀ *Silver and gold powder from AMACO*
- ❀ *Stickpin jewelry findings*
- ❀ *Assorted beads from Beadworks; shown on page 18 from left to right: Japanese pink glass leaf on wire loop C11; lampwork ball beads with foil inserts: A21 in clear and pink (8mm) and C44 in turquoise and gold (10mm); gold ball chain CE; heavy metal beads: AP06 and AQ06*
- ❀ *Fine, short brads or thin headpins*
- ❀ *Blunt knife; metal cutters*
- ❀ *Pencil with eraser end; toothpicks*

Directions

Sculpting: Read "Working with Polymer Clay," below. These stickpin designs are free-form pieces, so refer to the photograph for ideas but experiment with clay colors, color combinations, and shapes. Shown here are mostly pea-sized (one large walnut-sized) pieces of clay formed into balls and cubes. Dip a finger into metallic powder and apply over some surfaces, and/or stack 2 different shapes and colors.

Assembly: If the stickpin finding ends with a perpendicular disk, bend the wire stem, making the stickpin all on one plane. Pierce balls and cubes of clay with the top of the stickpin, and smooth over the openings. Slightly flatten the front and back surfaces of the clay.

Adding Beads: For the glass leaf, simply insert the wire loop into the clay. Beads may also be secured by pressing them halfway into the clay, like the silver barrel bead at the center of the stickpin on the right.

The ball chain was also simply wrapped around the clay, trimmed with clippers to the desired length, and pressed so it sinks into the clay. To attach beads at the top, use brads or trim headpins with clippers so they may be inserted through one or more beads and into the clay. Make contrast-color beads from clay. Consider inserting the heads of brads or headpins into the clay, for studs.

Making Impressions: Use the eraser end of a pencil, perhaps dipped into metallic powder, to press circles into the clay. Use toothpicks to make stripes or swirls.

Finishing: Bake and cool the clay as directed. You may add metallic powder after baking, but you will need to seal it with a clear topcoat. ☽

Working With Polymer Clay

In this book, we have mostly used Sculpey III Modeling Compound and Fimo Modeling Material, also known as polymer clay, and hereafter referred to simply as clay. The former is softer, easier to work with; children and older people will have no difficulty using Sculpey. While Fimo is harder and more crumbly until you knead it, and takes more strength and patience to work with it, its final effect is stronger, less prone to cracking after baking, more durable and long-lasting. I recommend staying with the modeling compound indicated in the Materials & Tools list to obtain the best results for each project.

To knead the clay, work it with your fingers. Body heat warms the clay and makes it easier to manipulate. Knead the clay until it is soft and pliable. To make balls, roll it (in your palm for Fimo, on a tabletop for Sculpey). To make snakes, roll it between your hands or on a work surface—as appropriate to the clay. For special effects, twist 2 snakes in different colors together, wrap the twist around a solid disk, spiral it into a disk, or roll it into a ball. To roll out slabs, use a rolling pin (a fat, round primary-school pencil makes a great miniature rolling pin). For even slabs, place a piece of clay between two pieces of 3mm-thick balsa wood and press or roll from atop the layers. For polka dots, make tiny $1/16$" balls and adhere to a ball, snake, or slab. Leave them dimensional, or roll them until the surface is smooth.

You can find handy tools around the house: For cutting, use single-edge razor blades or paring knives; for sculpting and texturing the clay, use wood or metal skewers, toothpicks, tapestry needles. Designer Kathleen George recommends Colour Shapers, tools with soft rubber tips.

To bake pieces, place on a disposable aluminum pie pan, cookie sheet, or in a baking pan. Bake in a pre-heated oven set to 275° Fahrenheit for 15-20 minutes, depending on the size of the piece. Remove from oven and let cool for a few minutes before handling.

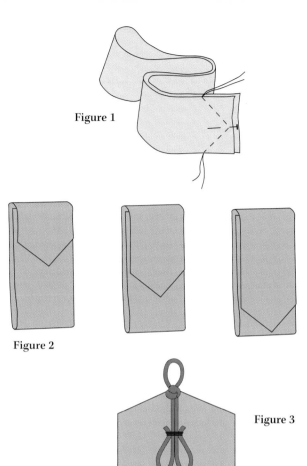

Figure 1

Figure 2

Figure 3

NECKLACE PURSES

Dimensions: Purses, not including necklace
strands, approximately 2″ by 3″

Materials & Tools

- *½ yard jacquard or brocade ribbon*
- *Medium or large bead: Venetian style lampwork
  clear teardrop bead D21 (shown here) and glass
  lampwork ball bead A 21 (8mm), from
  Beadworks*
- *Beads to coordinate with ribbon; shown here,
  from Mill Hill: 4 different colors of glass seed
  beads, one package pebble beads, a few bugle
  beads (optional)*
- *Sewing thread to match ribbon*
- *Optional closures: small scrap of elastic cord, or
  small snap*
- *Beading needle*
- *Sewing machine with zigzag stitch*

Directions

Sewing the purse: At or near one end of the ribbon,
identify a motif you would like centered on the flap.
Insert a pin to mark the exact center of the ribbon
where you would like the bottom of the V-shaped
flap. Fold the ribbon crosswise in half, right sides
facing, and use the same pin to pierce the center of
the ribbon at the other end. Using small straight
stitches, machine-stitch an even V across both
layers, as shown in figure 1.

Trim the seam, cutting close to stitches at the
center. Turn the ribbon to the right side, and finger-
press the seam. Using small zigzag stitches and
starting from the V, stitch along the long edges of the
ribbon, catching both layers and encasing the wrong
side completely. Fold this piece approximately into
thirds, with the V-flap on top. Try some different
folds, with one side showing, then with the reverse
side on the outside. Consider variations with the

19

straight end coming up higher, and the flap ends at the center. See figure 2 for variations. When you are satisfied with the amount of motif displayed on the flap and/or below the flap, pin the purse sides together with the flap flipped up, out of the way. Machine-zigzag-stitch the sides of the pursetogether, creating a pocket; leave the thread ends very long.

Making a Closure: For a loop that will fit over a ball bead, as shown on the black purse, fold elastic cord crosswise in half, and knot close to fold, leaving a small loop that will fit snugly over bead. Stitch knot at point of V on underside of flap. Finish ends of elastic cord neatly as shown in figure 3. Alternately, stitch on a snap to close the flap.

Beadwork: Thread a beading needle with sewing thread, either pulling thread's ends even with each other, or adding a second strand so that you always work with doubled thread. Bring the needle through the ribbon, starting about an inch away, and emerging where beading is to start. Make 2 or 3 tiny back-stitches or knots at the surface to secure thread at beginning and end of each strand of beading. Thread on beads in a repeated sequence. Always end a dangling strand with a seed bead. Always bring the needle back the same way, wrapping around the thread at the beginning of the bead sequence, going through the ribbon for a few inches for a well-anchored tail end. Clip threads close to the surface where they emerge.

Start by decorating the pointed end of flap. In the case of the snap closure (beige purse), beading is done at the tip of the flap itself, with pebble and teardrop beads first and foremost. Proceed from those beads in adding three dangling strands, each about 2" in length and made up mostly of seed beads, with an occasional, randomly-placed bugle bead added. Pebble beads were used at the bottom of each strand. In the case of a loop (black purse), first sew on a large ball bead (ending with a seed bead) for the loop to catch. Stitch three dangling strands from the base of the ball bead. Instead of bugle beads, a color sequence may be used to further distinguish the dangling strands.

Make use of existing thread ends to do the following beadwork whenever possible. Decorate the bottom of the purse with three loops of seed beads, with a center loop hanging about 2" below the ribbon and loops to either side hanging about 1/4" long. Optionally, make a scalloped edging on the flap consisting of shallow loops. Finally, make the necklace. Determine how long you want this necklace, and use existing threads only if they are long enough. Otherwise, fasten thread securely at top of pocket on one side to begin, at other side to end. Use seed beads in a repeated sequence, referring to the photograph for suggestions. Thread a needle with any remaining threads, weave them into the machine stitches, and clip the excess. ✣

ROMANTIC ACCENTS

Dimensions: 2½" by 2¾", not including the dangling fringe

Materials & Tools

- ❦ Seed beads and bugle beads from Mill Hill, as designated on the key
- ❦ DMC 6-strand embroidery floss; see the key for colors
- ❦ Silk embroidery ribbon, 4mm; see the key for colors
- ❦ Small amount of Mill Hill 14-count perforated paper in ecru (for Midnight Rose design) or white (for Morning Rose design)
- ❦ Jewelry finding for back of piece
- ❦ Glue
- ❦ Tapestry (#24) and beading (#10) needles
- ❦ Small sharp scissors

General Directions

Preparation: Cut a sheet of perforated paper crosswise in half; use one half for each design. Measure and lightly pencil-mark the center on the right side: the smooth side of the perforated paper. Each intersection on the chart represents a hole on the perforated paper. Do not cut out the shape until all the stitching is completed.

Stitching: Work each piece as charted, referring to the key and working in the following order: First, embroider with floss, then work the ribbon embroidery, then add the beads, except for the dangling fringe. Refer to the stitch details shown here, and to pages 124-125 for the remaining stitches.

Embroidery and Ribbon Embroidery: Use a tapestry needle. For ribbon embroidery, use 12″ lengths of ribbon. Thread the end of the ribbon through the eye of the needle. Pierce this end of the ribbon with the point of the needle directly in the center of the ribbon and ¾″ from the far end. Pull the ribbon through until it is firmly locked in the eye of the needle. To begin stitching, anchor the ribbon as follows: Hold 1″ of ribbon on the back of the work and carefully pierce the center of the ribbon when you take the first stitch. To end a piece of ribbon, weave the end into worked stitches on the back, then clip the excess ribbon.

Beadwork: Use a beading needle with 2 strands of floss for beading. If you have difficulty putting 2 strands of floss into the eye of the beading needle, put one strand through the eye and pull the thread ends even to double the working strand. Carefully separate beads, matching colors to the description. Some shades are close in color. Keep the small quantity of beads you are working with in a small glass or plastic dish with a slight rim. Do not take more beads from the container than you intend to use at one time—it's a lot easier to take them out than to put them back into the container! With counted bead embroidery that is, all work with seed beads except for bead loop flowers and five-bead posy—

use half-cross stitches, attaching a bead before completing each stitch. Refer to "How to Cross Stitch," on page 125. Make all of these stitches go in the same direction, so the beads lay properly. To move to another area, do not jump more than 3 or 4 holes without first securing the thread on the back.

Add the small (6mm) bugle beads using a long cross stitch (see diagram). Add the medium (8mm) bugle beads with a long straight stitch, passing through the bead twice for durability and security.

Cutting: After all stitching and beading is done, cut out the shape one hole beyond the stitched area. Be especially careful not to clip a working thread along curves and corners.

Adding the Dangling Fringe: Refer to the letters or dots at the bottom of the chart, and add the fringes to the bottom of the piece, using 1 strand of floss. Go through the sequence indicated, then return up through these beads starting with the fourth bead. This will form a 3-bead picot at the bottom of each fringe. Adjust and fasten each fringe before going on to the next fringe.

Finishing: Glue on a pin back, short barrette, bola finding, shoe clip, or other jewelry finding. Allow glue to dry.

MIDNIGHT ROSE DESIGN

Stitching: Follow chart, key, and general directions.

Adding Bead Loops: At each large diamond symbol, pick up 7 champagne beads, return the needle through the first bead and down in the same hole to form a loop. Adjust each loop before going on to the next one.

Fringe: At each dot, add a fringe at the bottom of the piece, using 1 strand of dark peach floss. Return up through these beads starting with the black bugle. Make sure each fringe is adjusted before going to the next fringe. Bead sequence:

For the 3 outer fringes on each side: 2 petite champagne, 1 metallic rose, 1 nutmeg bugle, 1 metallic rose, 2 petite champagne, 1 metallic rose, 1 black bugle, 1 petite champagne, 1 metallic rose, 1 petite champagne.

For the center 3 fringes: 2 petite champagne, 1 metallic rose, 1 black bugle, 1 metallic rose, 2 petite champagne, 1 metallic rose, 1 black bugle, 3 metallic rose.

ROMANTIC ACCENTS
continued

ALICIA LACE
Work in diagonal rows in running stitch. Work all stitches in one direction and then return in the other direction.

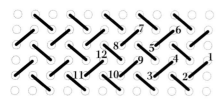

5-BEAD POSY
This is merely a beaded cross stitch. On the 1-2 stitch, pick up 2 Champagne Ice beads. On the 3-4 stitch, pick up 1 Champagne Ice, 1 Metallic Rose, 1 Champagne Ice. When you go down at 4, tuck the middle bead in the center using tight tension to pop it in place.

STITCHING SMALL BUGLE BEADS
Make a long cross stitch as shown.

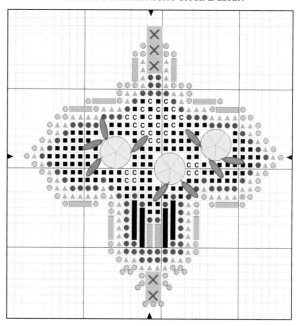

KEY

Half Cross Stitch with 6 Strands of Floss
▲ Dark Peach #407
■ Black #310

Ribbonwork
⊛ Spider web roses using Dark Peach #407 floss for spokes, light peach and peach ribbon combined for weaving
⟋ Lazy daisy stitch with green silk ribbon

Beadwork Applied with Dark Peach #407 Floss
C Bead loops with Champagne Ice #03050
○ Champagne Ice #03050
● Metallic Rose #03005
✕ 5-Bead Posy with Champagne Ice #03050 and Metallic Rose #03005
○ Petite Champagne #42027
▬ Black Bugle #82014
▬ Nutmeg Bugle #72053

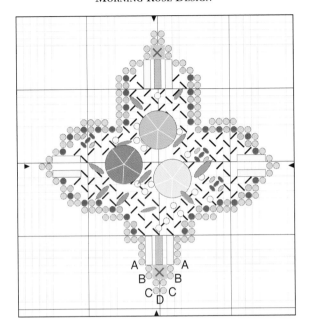

MORNING ROSE DESIGN

Stitching: Follow chart, key, and general directions.
Adding Bead Loop Flowers: At each dot on chart, pick up 1 mauve and 8 petite cream beads, then return the needle through the first bead and down into the same hole to form a loop. Adjust each loop before going on to the next one. Add a metallic rose bead to the center of each group of bead loops.
Fringe: Referring to the letters at the bottom of the chart and to the general directions, add fringes to the bottom of the piece, using 1 strand of white floss and making a picot at the bottom of each. Bead sequence:

A—1 metallic rose, 2 petite cream, 1 bay leaf, 1 petite cream, 1 bay leaf, 3 petite cream, 1 metallic rose, 1 nutmeg bugle, 1 metallic rose, 3 petite cream, 1 metallic rose, 3 bay leaf, 3 petite cream.

B—1 metallic rose, 2 petite cream, 3 bay leaf, 3 petite cream, 1 metallic rose, 3 petite cream, 2 bay leaf, 3 petite cream.

C—1 metallic rose, 2 petite cream, 1 bay leaf, 2 petite cream, 1 metallic rose, 2 petite cream, 1 mauve, 1 sm. cream bugle, 1 mauve, 2 petite cream, 1 bay leaf, 3 petite cream.

D—1 metallic rose, 3 petite cream, 1 metallic rose, 1 nutmeg bugle, 1 metallic rose, 3 petite cream, 1 metallic rose, 3 bay leaf, 3 petite cream. ✧

KEY

Stitchery with Floss
/ Alicia Lace with 4 strands of floss in Light Green #503
/ Lazy daisy stitch with 6 strands of floss in Medium Green #3815

Ribbonwork: Spider web roses using white floss for spokes
⊛ Dark pink and medium pink silk ribbon
⊛ Off-white and medium pink silk ribbon
○ Off-white and dark pink silk ribbon

Beadwork applied with white floss
○ Bay Leaf #03055
○ Champagne #03050
● Metallic Rose #03005
✕ 5-bead posy with Champagne #03050 and Metallic Rose #03005 (Metallic Rose centers)
○ Bead loop flowers with Petite Cream #40123
▭ Cream bugle #70123
▭ Nutmeg bugle #82053

FLOWERPOT PIN CUSHION

Dimensions: 3″ high

Materials & Tools

- *Offray wired ribbons, 1½″ wide: ½ yard Metallic Ombre #6571, Comb. 5¾ yard Ombre #6348 in Comb. 21*
- *Matching sewing thread*
- *3 cotton balls, or a bit of polyester fiberfill*
- *Terra cotta mini flowerpot, 1⅝″ high and in diameter at the rim*

continued

- ❧ *Copper paint*
- ❧ *Small stones*
- ❧ *Sewing needle*
- ❧ *Paintbrush*
- ❧ *Glue gun and glue stick*

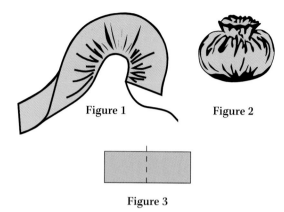

Figure 1   Figure 2

Figure 3

Figure 4   Figure 5

Directions

Making the Bud: Cut 1½″ from one end of metallic ombre ribbon and set aside. On remaining ombre ribbon, pull wire ends to remove wire completely from one long edge, and to gather the ribbon tightly along the opposite long edge (see figure 1). Wrap wire ends together to form a ring. Where the wire was removed, make running stitches using a needle and doubled thread, ¼″ from edge. Gather these stitches loosely but do not fasten off thread. Insert cotton balls or fiberfill to stuff the bud, covering them with the cut off ribbon square. Pull gathers tightly as you can to nearly close the bud, then fasten off the thread. See figure 2.

Making the Leaves: Cut 4½″ lengths of green ribbon for each of 5 leaves. Visually divide the piece crosswise in half (see figure 3), then fold the top corners diagonally to the center (figure 4). Stitch along the lower edge and gather tightly, then fasten off the thread. Trim excess ribbon below the gathers (figure 5). Sew on leaves with their raw edges tucked under the bottom of the bud, so they radiate outward all around.

Assembly: Paint the exterior of the flowerpot. Glue the largest stone over the opening in the bottom, and fill three-quarters full with stones. Hot-glue the bud into the top of the pot, pressing down until the glue sets. Curl each leaf down over the rim, then bend the tips upward. ❧

NEEDLEPOINT BROOCH

shown on page 13

Dimensions: Design area, 1⅝″ by 1¼″; mounted in the frame as shown, 2¼ by 1⅞″

Materials & Tools

- ❧ *Small piece of Congress Cloth, from Zweigart*
- ❧ *Silk and wool Impressions by Caron from The Caron Collection, 1 skein each color listed in the Color Key*
- ❧ *Kreinik #8 Fine Braid, 1 skein each color listed in the Color Key*
- ❧ *Antique Gold Oval Brooch #AG17 from Anne Brinkley Designs*
- ❧ *Craft glue*
- ❧ *#26 tapestry needle*
- ❧ *Stretcher bars or small needlework frame (optional)*

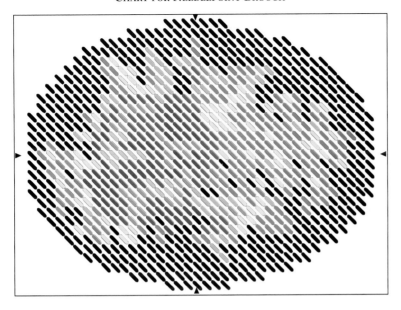

KEY

Impressions
- Salmon
- Burgundy
- Cherry
- Lavendar
- Emerald
- Sage Green
- Pale Celadon
- Yellow
- Black

Kreinik Fine Braid #8
- Orchid
- Bahama Blue #329
- Garnet #080HL
- Fuchsia #024

Directions

Stitching: Turn chart sideways to work stitches in the proper direction. Needlepoint on canvas following the chart and key. Work in continental stitch, referring to the Needlepoint Know-How on page 17. Separate strands of Impressions and use one strand only throughout the project.

Assembly: Cut out canvas just slightly beyond outer row of stitches. Follow the manufacturer's instructions to insert needlepoint into the brooch frame.

RIBBON EMBROIDERY BROOCH

shown on page 12

Dimensions: 1⅞″ by 1½″

Materials & Tools

- Small piece of heavy silk, moire, or satin fabric in fuchsia (Note: If fabric is lightweight, fuse a thin interfacing to the back)
- Bucilla 100% Silk Ribbon, 4mm wide: Hot Pink #552, Dark Green #629, Pale Green #651, and Orchid #204
- Kreinik Fine Braid #8 in Confetti Fuchsia #042
- 1 package Mill Hill Glass Treasures #12187: blue flowers
- 7 Beadworks round 3mm amethyst-faceted beads
- Sewing thread in pink, aqua
- Scrap of thin batting
- Framecraft oval brooch frame BO2, 1⅞″ x 1½″ in gold, from Mill Hill
- Fade-out pen (used here, Duncan Disappearing Ink pen)
- Chenille, sewing, and beading needles
- Optional: ¼ yard ombre wire edge ribbon, ⅞″ wide

Directions

Marking the Design: Photocopy the actual-size pattern. Place the fabric over the copied pattern and pin edges to secure. Hold these layers over a well-lit window, and go over a few important lines and dots with fade-out pen. Be prepared to work the piece directly afterwards because these guidelines will fade away. You may, however, reapply markings if necessary. Refer to the photo and pattern when adding embellishments.

RIBBON EMBROIDERY BROOCH
continued

Ribbon Embroidery: Refer to the stitch details on pages 124-125, the actual-size pattern below, and the key for stitches, colors, and placements. Work stitches in the following order and colors: Begin with an orchid spider web rose, using pink thread for the spokes, and then orchid French knot buds. Next, work the dark green Japanese ribbon stitch leaves, the pale green French knot buds, and lastly, the hot pink Japanese ribbon stitch leaves.

Embroidery: Couch fine braid along the lines of the bow, using aqua sewing thread.

Beadwork: Sew faceted and flower beads in place using matching thread.

Finishing: Position the clear plastic window from the frame over the stitchery, trace around it, and cut out the design. Also cut two small ovals of batting: one the same size, another $1/8''$ smaller all around. Place the smaller, then the same-size batting ovals behind the fabric. Follow the manufacturer's instructions to mount needlework in the frame and attach the backing (a pinback is included). Insert a bow of ombre wire edge ribbon if desired. ✤

ACTUAL-SIZE PATTERN

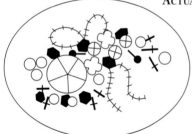

	Orchid spider web rose
	Orchid French knot buds
	Dark Green Japanese ribbon stitch
	Pale Green French knot buds
	Hot Pink Japanese ribbon stitch
	Couching Fine Braid with aqua thread
	Blue flower beads
	Amethyst faceted beads

MESSAGE COMBS

Dimensions: 3" across

Materials & Tools

- ✤ Crystal (clear plastic) hair combs
- ✤ Bucilla 100% silk variegated ribbon, $1/2''$ wide, one 2-yard package for each pair of combs: Terra Cotta #1314, and Olive Green #1311
- ✤ Pearl beads, 5mm
- ✤ Assortment of buttons and ribbon roses; shown here, ready-made assortments: Dress It Up Buttons-N-Bows (Peaches & Cream) #105 and Heirloom Collection #77
- ✤ Tapestry needle
- ✤ Mini hot glue gun and glue sticks
- ✤ Optional: Gold-plated angel charms; clock parts that are no longer in working order; these are from wristwatches; clear tape or self adhesive vinyl

Directions

Covering the Comb: Lay one end of ribbon across the back of the comb at the top. Bring ribbon around the end of the comb, between the first and second teeth, and lay it flatly over the top of the comb. Bring it around and between the second and third teeth. Wrap it again over the top. Continue wrapping the top of the comb in this manner. When you reach the other end of the comb, cut the ribbon, leaving a 3" tail with an angled end. Insert a tapestry needle under a few ribbon wraps on the back, thread the eye with the tail, and pull the tail through. Trim the ribbon close to the surface where it emerges. Wrap the second comb in the same way.

Make a bow: Divide the remaining ribbon in half; use one strand for each comb. Tie a simple bow. Glue the bow off-center to the top of the comb, or fold the bow crosswise in half and glue it to one end of the comb, with loops and streamer ends radiating outward. Clip the streamer ends at an angle.

Type messages: Photocopy the lines below, or type your own descriptive phrase onto a home computer. Format the phrase in a pretty font; shown here is French Script MT in 18 point bold letters. Cut out the phrase, leaving ¼″ all around. Laminate the message with clear tape or clear self-adhesive vinyl and trim close to the letters at top and bottom only. Notch the side edges to form an outward point. Insert these points into the ribbon wraps, squeezing a dot of hot glue under the message at the center.

Adding Embellishments: Glue clock parts, charms, ribbon roses, buttons, and pearls across the top of the comb. Use tweezers to prevent fingers from coming into contact with hot glue. Start with the largest items and work down to the smallest, filling in gaps with single pearls. Also glue pearls to center of buttons, if desired. ◊

MESSAGES
TO PHOTOCOPY

Dreamer

Poetry in Motion

SHOE EMBELLISHMENTS

Dimensions of motif: 1 ½″ by 2″

Materials & Tools

- ❦ *Scrap of synthetic suede to match suede shoes*
- ❦ *Bucilla 100% Silk Ribbon in 13mm Variegated Ice Cream #1308, and 7mm Dark Seafoam #625*
- ❦ *Bucilla Organza Ribbon in 18mm Pale Pink #1503*
- ❦ *Ivory pearls, 3mm, from Sulyn Industries*
- ❦ *Pale pink sewing thread*
- ❦ *Aleene's Tacky Glue*
- ❦ *Chenille needle*
- ❦ *Iron*
- ❦ *Optional: Purchased shoe clips to cover*

Directions for Each:

Preparation: From synthetic suede, cut a ¾″ x 1½″ rectangle; round the corners. Lightly press all the ribbons.

Making the Buds: Hold the organza ribbon over the 13mm variegated ribbon, and follow the directions and diagrams for leaves on the Flowerpot Pincushion on page 24. Make 3 buds in this way. Turn the raw edges under and stitch the buds to the suede piece, following the diagram and photograph for placement, and placing the center bud first, the others overlapping it.

Stitching: For sepals, use a chenille needle and dark seafoam ribbon to stitch Japanese ribbon stitches to bases of buds. Refer to the ribbon embroidery stitches on page 124, and to the actual-size diagram for the length of stitches. Sew approximately 14 pearls in place at the base of the Japanese ribbon stitches.

Finishing: Trim away excess synthetic suede. Glue the suede piece to a shoe clip, or directly onto a shoe. ◊

ACTUAL-SIZE DIAGRAM
FOR SHOE EMBELLISHMENT

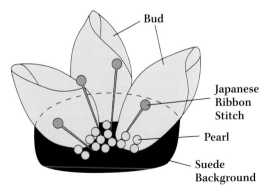

Bud

Japanese
Ribbon
Stitch

Pearl

Suede
Background

27

Chapter Two

Keepsakes

At the turn of the century, the Russian Tsars bestowed the most fabulously elaborate enameled eggs from the studios of Faberge upon members of their royal court. These little eggs opened—sometimes to reveal a painted interior or a miniature palace, or perhaps a coach pulled by tiny horses. Invariably, however, they served as elaborate bibelots rather than as functional objects of containment.

 A beautiful miniature box might serve to hold an expensive piece of jewelry or a tiny seashell. Or it might contain only dreams or memories. This and other tokens for display make perfect gifts. No one can say they don't have the room for one—it takes up hardly any space. By virtue of their diminutive dimensions they  may be kept out and admired. And the sentiments or the sentimental memories that accompany them elevate their value far beyond their visual charms.

Presentments

Designer Kathleen George's versatility is aptly demonstrated by the various styles reflected in these pieces: From left, the standing frame is Art Deco, the ornate hanging clock is Rococo, the open box to hold business cards, inlaid with the tiniest seashells, is Art Nouveau, and the graceful, classical swirls of the easel stand identify it as Baroque. Fimo modeling compound was the medium behind each piece.

Gentle reader, you are doubtless aware that your local photocopy shop will reduce any old photographs to fit a small frame. You can perch them upon a tiny easel stand, or set them, instead of a clock, into the face of a hanging frame, or make them part of a collection in a tiny box. You may also wish to create your artwork for display. On the easel stand, Kathleen showcases a mini frame purchased from any crafts or miniatures store. She gave an antique patina to the plastic frame with a fingertip of aqua acrylic paint, and inserted a card-stock rectangle to which she had glued some pressed flowers. Voila! A still-life masterpiece.

Imagination Is Served

Almost no one takes a small cup of strong black coffee after dinner, but who wouldn't covet a collection of demitasse cups that hold new expressions of sentiment? Kathleen George lavished these cups with ribbons from Mokuba, pin-weaving them for a pin cushion, ruching them to ring a cache of potpourri, or fanning them out and forming cockades around a candle cup. Kathleen saw the demitasse in a new light as well: by inverting the cup and placing a floral arrangement in the saucer, she created a magical, miniature birdbath.

I Think That I Shall Never See...

Like Faberge eggs, these oval boxes may contain nothing but memories and dreams. Their lids portray a landscape of the mind—or perhaps of reality. Trips to Italy, to the Pacific Northwest, and to my own backyard inspired these images. My needlework technique of choice, free-motion embroidery, allows me to

"paint" in very quick strokes with rayon and metallic threads, using the sewing machine. Simply drop the feed dogs and attach a darning foot to your machine. With a bit of practice, anyone who enjoys sewing can create a miniature work of art. Gold and silver markers added rich pattern to the elegant china boxes.

Tokens of Affection

Valentines need not be two-dimensional works in paper, nor need they be reserved for any one day of the year. A delicacy of scale, the sweet motif of heart or rose, and Victoriana references transform each of these objects into a hallmark of sentiment. Kathryn Severns fashioned the twig chair and loveseat from a single grapevine wreath, soaking and re-shaping the vines to her will. At far left and far right, boxes from American Traditional Stencils were painted with mini brass stencils on delicately mottled

backgrounds. A diamond shape of iridescent beads tops a tiny round crystal box from Mill Hill, the perfect container for an engagement ring. Almost like china, the rectangular gift box is actually thin slabs and moldings of Fimo; it's by Kathleen George. A trio of soft hearts may hold potpourri, to serve as sachets in lingerie drawers or clothes hangers. Or they may serve as reliquaries, stuffed with rice or flower petals from a wedding. Penny Kimball cross-stitched each long-stemmed rose and floral vine using rayon floss from DMC.

Materials & Tools

- Fimo* Modeling Material (hereafter referred to as "clay") 1 package each Fir Green, Lilac, Violet
- Red and blue metallic powders*
- Scrap of thin leather or synthetic suede, for hinge
- ⅝" bugle bead
- Epoxy glue
- Small piece of black paper, for mat
- Photo or picture
- Clear tape
- Rolling pin
- Balsa wood sheets
- Craft knife
- Cutting mat

*From AMACO

ART DECO
PICTURE FRAME

Dimensions: 3¼" by 3¼" by 3" deep

Directions

Preparation: Photocopy patterns twice. Cut out pieces for front, back, and decorative strips and swirls separately. Read and refer to "Working with Polymer Clay" on page 18 and refer to the photograph.

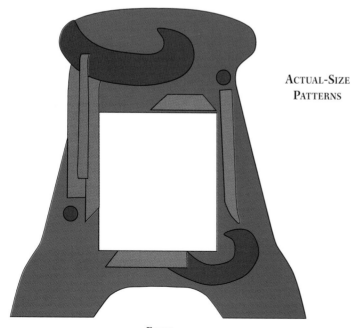

ACTUAL-SIZE
PATTERNS

Front

Back

Cutting and Baking: Roll out fir green clay in a sheet $^3/_{16}''$ thick. Use Front and (easel stand) Back patterns to cut out the main frame pieces. Roll out a small amount of violet and lilac clay, making them a bit thinner. Rub a mixture of blue and red metallic powders on the lilac clay. Use swirl patterns to cut out pieces from violet clay, and straight pattern strips to cut out pieces from metallic-tinted lilac clay. Lay these shapes on the Front frame piece as shown. Add two tiny balls of violet clay, piercing them with a pin to facilitate good adhesion. Bake according to the package instructions and let cool.

Assembly: Cut a $1'' \times {}^3/_4''$ rectangle of leather. Fold it crosswise in half and glue one half to the underside of the frame Front, other half to the underside of the frame's Back. Let dry. Glue a bugle bead along the top of the leather at the fold, to simulate a hinge.

Providing a Picture Insert: Using a craft knife and ruler, cut a $1^3/_4'' \times 1^7/_8''$ rectangle with a ${}^7/_8'' \times 1^1/_8''$ window opening from black paper, for a mat. Use a photocopier to reduce a photograph to fit inside the window opening. Use clear tape to adhere the picture behind the mat, and both behind the window opening of the frame. ⚓

- ✄ *Tapestry needle*
- ✄ *Electric frying pan for heating water*
- ✄ *Jewelry (small needlenose) pliers*

*From AMACO

ROCOCO CLOCK

Dimensions: $2^1/_2''$ by $3''$, not including hanging and dangling chains

Materials & Tools

- ✄ *Friendly Plastic*: 3 sticks each Pewter, Flat Gold, and Deep Rose (fuchsia)*
- ✄ *Small clock face (as shown, from a wristwatch)*
- ✄ *Gold angel charm, $2^1/_2'' \times 1^1/_8''$*
- ✄ *2 gold filigree beads, 6mm*
- ✄ *2 silver beads, 4mm*
- ✄ *18'' of fine gold chain*
- ✄ *2 gold eye pins*
- ✄ *3 fuchsia rhinestones, 3mm*
- ✄ *Friendly Plastic Arts & Craft Goop**
- ✄ *Wide cloth tape*
- ✄ *Small Roses Push Mold**

Directions

Softening Friendly Plastic: Heat water and keep it hot but not boiling. Use tongs or tweezers to submerge small pieces of Friendly Plastic for a few minutes. Once the Friendly Plastic is removed from the hot water, work with it quickly. If it starts to harden before you are finished manipulating its shape, dip it into the hot water for 2 or 3 minutes again.

Framing the Clock: Cut two ${}^5/_8'' \times 2^1/_2''$ strips from both pewter and gold Friendly Plastic. Soften the strips and lay the pewter ones overlapping the top and bottom of the clock face, the gold ones along the sides, crisscrossing each other. The Friendly Plastic will not stick to the watch face. Remove the watch and set it aside while you finish the frame.

Making Embellishments: Trace the shape of the angel charm onto pewter Friendly Plastic. Cut out the shape, soften it, and attach it to the top of the clock frame. Immediately press the angel charm firmly onto the shape. Make 1 large rose and 2 small roses by softening small pieces of pewter Friendly Plastic and pressing them immediately into the rose mold. Make 2 small gold leaves in the same manner. From fuchsia Friendly Plastic, hand-cut 2 slender leaves, about 1″ in length. Soften them and position them below the window opening of the frame as shown. Cut out two 3/16″ x 1¼″ strips of Friendly Plastic for ribbons. Cut one end of each on an angle. Soften these, and apply them to the center top of the frame, curving gently down over the angel charm. Cut two 1″ x 2″ rectangles of gold Friendly Plastic. Soften them, and roll them into tubes. While the plastic is still soft, use a needle to press lines lengthwise into the sides, to simulate fluted columns.

Assembly: Use Goop to adhere beads, roses, leaves, columns and rhinestones, referring to the photograph for suggested placements. Glue an eye pin on the back of the horizontal Friendly Plastic pewter strip at each bottom corner, with the eye extending below the strip. Cut a 2½″ length of chain. Glue the ends to the back, at the top and ¾″ apart, for hanging. Let the glue dry thoroughly. For a double swag, cut a 6″ and a 6½″ length of chain. Using jewelry pliers, open one eye of the eye pins and insert a chain link 1¼″ from the end of each length of chain. Close the eye to secure the chains. Repeat with the other eye pin and the opposite ends of the chains.

Insert the clock face into position from the back. Apply cloth tape over the back to hold the clock in place. Unpeel the backing when needed to change the time or replace the batteries. At that time, apply a fresh piece of tape to the back. ✧

Materials & Tools

- ✤ Fimo Modeling Material* (hereafter referred to as "clay"), in Caramel
- ✤ Red, Blue, and Silver Metallic Powders*
- ✤ Assortment of tiny shells and sea treasures
- ✤ A few green Antique Glass Seed Beads from Mill Hill
- ✤ Friendly Plastic Arts & Craft Goop*
- ✤ Craft knife
- ✤ Cutting mat
- ✤ Cookie sheet
- ✤ Metal-edge ruler
- ✤ Straight pin

*From AMACO

Directions

Preparation: Read and refer to "Working with Polymer Clay" on page 18. Roll out a thin sheet of caramel clay, ¼″ thick. Cut out a box bottom, 1″ x 3⅞″, and two sides, 1″ square. Trace and cut out the actual-size patterns. Use the patterns to cut out the Front and Back pieces.

Applying Patina: Cover all areas that will show with metallic powders as follows: Begin by applying very small dots of blue and red metallic powder with your fingertip. Rub them gently and thoroughly into the surface of the clay. Then rub a thin layer of silver metallic powder all over the surface of the clay, and rub gently with your fingertip until the clay has a satin-like sheen. The trick is to apply a light dusting of powder each time, so that the colors shine through each other.

Embellishing: Place the two side pieces and the bottom piece on a cookie sheet. Press a single

ART NOUVEAU BUSINESS CARD HOLDER

Dimensions: 3⅞″ by 1⅜″ deep by 2⅛″ high

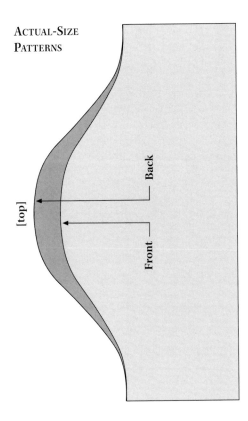

[top]

Back

Front

BAROQUE
EASEL STAND

Dimensions: $2\frac{1}{4}''$ by $4''$ by $2\frac{1}{2}''$ deep

Materials & Tools

- Black Fimo Modeling Material from AMACO, hereafter referred to as "clay"
- $\frac{5}{8}''$ hematine cabochon (silvery, oval jewel)
- 3 silver eye pins
- 2 silver beads, 4mm
- $1\frac{1}{2}''$ length of fine silver chain
- 2 tiny jump rings
- Craft knife
- Cutting mat
- Jewelry (needlenose) pliers

Directions

Preparation: Read and refer to "Working with Polymer Clay" on page 18. Roll out a thin sheet of clay, $1\frac{1}{4}''$ thick.

Cutting: Cut out $\frac{1}{4}''$ strips to the following lengths: two $4''$, and one each $3\frac{1}{2}''$ and $1''$. Trace the actual-size patterns for the crossbar and picture rest, and use to cut pieces.

Assembly: Temporarily wedge the $1''$ strip between the $4''$ strips, for front legs. Join the crossbar seamlessly between the $4''$ legs, $1''$ from the bottom, with the long straight edge on top. Embellish the picture rest as follows: Curl in the ends and press the cabochon to the center. Encircle with slender snakes of clay with curlicued ends. Press the picture rest to

favorite shell into the Back piece of the box, and place that on the cookie sheet as well. For the Front of the box, score lines to break the space into a crazy quilt-type design, using the edge of the craft knife and a ruler. Press down very slightly to create a line, but do not cut through the clay. Within these divided areas, create a variety of textures with other tools and materials, such as the head of a straight pin, a needle, or the knife blade. Whether the texture is a dotted stippling, scratchy lines, or little curlicues, keep it subtle. Press odds and ends of small seashore materials into the clay as you wish. Press in a row of seed beads. Be aware that flat objects may have to be glued on after baking. Add the Front to the cookie sheet, and check to make sure all edges are straight and all angles are 90º before baking.

Finishing: Bake the pieces according to manufacturer's instructions. When cool, glue the box together using Goop glue. If necessary, glue on any items that came off in the baking. ◊

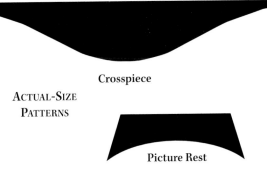

Crosspiece

Picture Rest

41

BAROQUE EASEL STAND
continued

the crossbar with the straight edges aligned. Add tiny balls at the top of each easel leg, and also a slender, curlicued snake that bridges the 4″ legs on top.

Carefully insert a needle through the top of the 4″ legs of the easel, with the 1″ piece in between. Carefully remove the needle, and the 1″ strip. Make a hole through the top of the 3½″ leg as well. A connecting eye pin will travel through these holes. Place all pieces on a cookie sheet and bake at about 275 ° Fahrenheit for 15 minutes. Let cool.

Thread an eye pin with a silver bead, run the eye pin through the holes of the three easel legs and add a silver bead at the other side. Snip the eye pin ¼″ beyond the bead hole and bend the end around to secure. Trim the shanks of two other eye pins to ¼″. Gently twist one eye pin into the back of the crosspiece behind the picture rest, and the other to the front of the center leg, 1¾″ from the bottom. Use the pliers to open the eyes of the pins and attach the ends of the chain. ◊

DEMITASSES

Dimensions: Cups, 2″ to 2½″ in diameter; saucers, about 4½″ in diameter; total arrangements, 2½″ to 4″ in height

PINCUSHION
Materials

- ✧ *Mokuba Ribbons: 1¼ yards each of the following, for pin-weaving: Black, ochre and gold jacquard #4537, color 14, ½″ wide; black and gold stripe #4594, color 95, ¼″ wide; olive jacquard #4593, color 17, ⅜″ wide. For ruffle, 1⅝ yards sheer green ribbon #4596, color 17, ⅝″ wide. For bow on cup handle, ⅝ yard sheer green ribbon with gold center stripe #4597, color 14, ⅝″ wide*
- ✧ *Sheffield demitasse cup and saucer, by Spode, from Royal China & Porcelain*
- ✧ *Sewing thread in a color to match ribbons*
- ✧ *5″ square of fusible interfacing*
- ✧ *Black felt, 2½″ diameter circle*
- ✧ *Small amount of polyester fiberfill, for stuffing*
- ✧ *Cardboard or matboard*
- ✧ *Straight pins and sewing needle*
- ✧ *Iron*

Directions

Pin-weaving: Lay the square of fusible interfacing with the fusible, or rough side, up on top of the cardboard. For a warp, cut the ½″ wide ribbons into 8 strips, 5″ in length. Arrange them vertically side by side and right side up on the interfacing. Place pins into the ribbon ends and the cardboard to temporarily secure the strands. For the weft, or weavers, cut six 5″ strips from both the ¼″ and ⅜″ wide ribbon. Weave a ¼″ wide ribbon over and under the warp strands, making one horizontal row all the way across. See figure 1. Remove and replace pins as needed, and secure the completed weft row with pins at either end. For a second horizontal row, weave a ⅜″ wide ribbon under, then over successive warp strands, creating a staggered pattern. See figure 2. Continue in this manner alternating all the

weft ribbons. Tighten up the spaces between the rows, to create a solid, interlaced fabric. Using a press cloth, iron the woven fabric to fuse the ribbons to the interfacing. Remove all the pins, turn the fabric to the wrong side and iron from this side to bond everything securely.

Making the Cushion: Cut the woven fabric into a 4″ circle. Use a needle with a double strand of sewing thread to sew a running stitch all around, ³⁄₈″ from the edges. Pull the thread ends to gather the circle loosely, fill it with a fistful of stuffing, and test-fit it in the demitasse cup. Adjust the stitches to make the ball tighter or looser for optimal fit. When it is the correct size and fullness, sew back and forth over the stuffing to secure it in place. Slip-stitch a 2¹⁄₂″ circle of felt over the bottom to conceal the fiberfill.

Making a Ruffle: Sew gathering stitches lengthwise along the center of the 1″ wide sheer ribbon. Pull the threads to adjust the gathers until the ruffle fits around the pincushion, then tack it in place all around.

Finishing: Secure the pincushion into the cup with white glue, if desired, or leave loose. Tie remaining sheer ribbon around the cup handle and form a simple bow. Cut ribbon ends on an angle. ✑

Figure 1

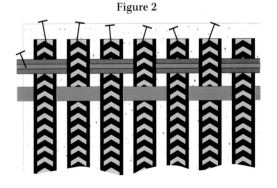

Figure 2

POTPOURRI HOLDER

Materials & Tools

- Mokuba Ribbons: For ruffle: 1⅜ yards purple with gold stripe border #4608, color 93, ⅝″ wide (A). For multi-loop bow: 1 yard blue #4599, color 2, ½″ wide (B); ⅝ yard sheer navy with gold edge #1520, color 19, ¹¹⁄₁₆″ wide (C); ⅜ yard purple silk #4595, color 4, ⅜″ wide (D); 2″ sheer blue with gold edge #4570, color 21, ⅝″ wide (E)
- Chancellor Cobalt demitasse cup and saucer, by Spode, from Royal China & Porcelain
- Blue sewing thread
- Pearl bead, 6mm
- ½ cup of potpourri
- Sewing needle
- Hot glue gun and glue stick

Directions

Making a Ruffle: Sew gathering stitches lengthwise along one edge of ribbon A. Bring the needle back to the beginning to form a ring, and pull the threads to adjust the gathers until the ruffle fits around the base of the cup. Make a few backstitches to secure the gathers.

Making a Multi-Loop Bow: For each individual bow, hold the ribbon indicated below 1½″ from one end. Make a loop the length indicated, and hold it with your thumb and forefinger. See figure 1. Make a second, same-size loop in the opposite direction. Hold both loops in the center with thumb and forefinger. Make a third loop to one side of the first loop. See figure 2. Continue to make loops, alternating sides. Thread a needle and tack a few stitches at the center to secure the bow.

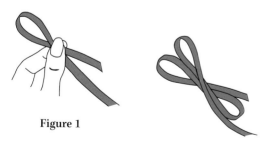

Figure 1

Figure 2

Using ribbon B, make a 6-loop bow with 1½″long loops. Using ribbon C, make a 6-loop bow with 1⅛″ long loops. Tie a simple bow with ribbon D, making the loops ¾″ in length. Stack the bows in B-C-D order, inserting one end of ribbon E between C and D, with all streamer ends at the bottom. Stitch the bows together at the center, adding a pearl to the top bow knot. Notch an inverted V into the end of ribbon E, and trim all other streamer ends on an angle.

Assembly: Attach the stacked bows to the cup below the handle using a dot of hot glue. Fill the cup with potpourri.

CANDLE CUP

Materials & Tools

- Mokuba Ribbons: 1 yard rust satin with sheer border #94598, color 9, ⅝″ wide; ½ yard blue satin with gold stripe border #4608, color 20, ⅝″ wide
- Colonel Blue demitasse cup and saucer by Spode, from Royal China & Porcelain
- 1 package Mill Hill Seed Beads in Rainbow #00374
- Rust sewing thread
- White craft glue
- Votive candle
- Beading needles

Directions

Making Cockades: Thread a beading needle with an 18″ length of sewing thread. Pull thread ends even, and knot the end. Cut rust ribbon into six 5″ lengths. For each cockade, stitch small running stitches ⅛″ from one long edge on a piece of ribbon. When you reach the end, pull the thread to gather the ribbon, and continue with a couple of stitches at the beginning of the strand, forming a ring. Pull the threads tightly to close the center, and make backstitches to secure. Do not clip the thread, but stitch about 8 seed beads separately to the center.

Arranging: Cut the blue ribbon into three 5″ lengths. Arrange two in a cross (X) formation, and lay the third across, like spokes of a wheel. Apply glue at the centers to secure them. Trim ribbon ends on the same angle all around. Lay these ribbon spokes across the saucer, with the cup on top. Arrange cockades in between spokes. Pour a tablespoon of water into the cup (to prevent melted wax from sticking), and insert a votive candle.

BIRDBATH CUP

Materials & Tools

- *Mokuba Ribbons:1 yard sheer green ribbon #4595, color 4, ⅝″ wide; ½ yard purple ribbon #4595, color 4, ⅜″ wide*
- *Sewing thread to match ribbons*
- *Warmstry White demitasse cup and saucer by Royal Worcester, from Royal China & Porcelain*
- *Tan air-drying modeling clay*
- *Small amounts of the following floral material: sphagnum moss, everlastings, green gyp, babies' breath*
- *Small amount of clean sand*
- *A handful of pebbles*
- *Envirotex Lite (a plastic which simulates water), from Environmental Technologies, Inc.*
- *Small mushroom bird, 2″ in length and 1″ high*
- *White craft glue*
- *Floral clay (optional)*
- *Sewing needle*
- *Paper cup and disposable stirrer*
- *Mini hot glue gun and glue stick*

Directions

Making the Birdbath: Line the saucer with a thin layer of modeling clay. Build up the area around the edge of the saucer with a roll of clay, in order to create a little well for "water" in the center. Press pebbles into the clay along the edges. Pat a bit of sand into the clay to cover the bottom of the well. Spread white glue on top of the clay surrounding the well, and pat on moss. Cut away most of the stems of several dried flowers, and insert these stems into the clay, clustering the florals along one half the mossy circle as shown, or as desired. Follow the directions on the EnviroTex Lite to prepare and pour the plastic into the well. Set this aside for 24 hours to harden.

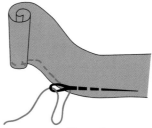

Figure 1

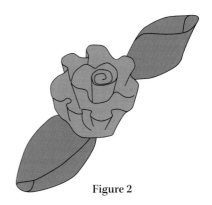

Figure 2

Making Ribbon Flowers: Create flowers as follows: Thread a needle with a double strand of purple sewing thread. Cut three 6″ lengths of purple ribbon. For each flower, make two tight wraps at one end of a ribbon length, to form a tube. Secure these wrappings at one end (this will be the bottom of the flower) with a few stitches. See figure 1. Make running stitches along the adjacent long edge, and pull the thread ends tightly to gather. As you do this, wrap the ribbon loosely around the tube, and tack it at the bottom to secure.

Using the green ribbon, create 6 leaves, following the directions for leaves as described in the Flowerpot Pincushion directions on page 24. Place the raw ends of 2 leaves under each flower, and stitch them together. See figure 2.

Finishing: Use a dab of hot glue to adhere the ribbon flowers among the dried flowers. At a point opposite the dried flowers, hot-glue the bird. Turn the cup upside down and set the saucer on top. If desired, insert a piece of floral clay in between to secure the arrangement. ⟡

LANDSCAPE BOXES

Dimensions: Lids, 2″ by 1½″; boxes, 1⅛″ high

Materials & Tools

- Framecraft porcelain boxes PL2, from Mill Hill, available in 11 colors; shown here: Soft Green, Burgundy, Blue, Ivory, Green
- Small amount (fat quarter) of light blue moiré fabric
- Small amount of Pellon Stitch-N-Tear rip-away backing
- Sulky threads: Original Metallic and 40-weight Rayon, one spool each color listed in the key, or colors as desired
- Light blue sewing thread
- Small amount of thin batting
- Formby's Decorative Touches gold and silver leaf pens
- Sewing machine with darning foot attachment
- Metafil sewing machine needle, size 14
- Black permanent ink marker (optional)
- Fade-out marker or dressmaker's marking pen
- Sewing needle

Directions

Preparation: Photocopy the design(s) of your choice. You may also use a photocopier to reduce a postcard, snapshot, or illustration to fit the oval design area. Go over the main design lines in fine black marker. Pin moiré fabric on top of the marked design, with the grain of the fabric on the horizontal, and with at least a 1″ margin all around. Hold this up to a sunny window and trace the design lines

that show through, using a fade-out marker or dressmaker's marking pen.

Free-Motion Stitchery: Practice these techniques on a scrap of moiré fabric before working on the marked design. Every machine is a bit different, and it takes experimenting to obtain just the right tension and become comfortable "drawing" with the sewing machine. You may also find it helpful to practice on a larger scale design first.

Tighten the bobbin tension. Loosen the top tension. Insert the darning foot attachment. Drop the feed dogs (usually, a button on the back of your machine; consult your sewing machine manual). Use a Metafil or top-stitch needle and a light blue sewing thread in the bobbin. With the stitch length at a medium setting (about 6 stitches to the inch), baste outside the design all around, securing the rip-away backing to the fabric. For all decorative stitching, set the machine almost to fine—about 14 stitches per inch. Try to start and end a color beyond the perimeter of the design area, or at the same place, to avoid threading so many ends to bring them to the wrong side.

Leave thread ends long, and before continuing to another color, thread ends onto a needle and bring them to the back of your work. When possible, work all areas of the same color before proceeding to another color. Stitch around the perimeter of the design to continue an area of color that meets the edge on another side.

For rows of grasses, stalks and blades, and other angular lines, use the zigzag stitch. For outlining, curlicues, or filling in colors, use a straight stitch. Work areas generally from background to foreground, or in this order: sun, skies, light-colored mountains, ice caps or dark mountain ridges, background plains, foreground plains, waterfall, river, pool of water, rocks in the foreground, tree trunk, leaves on the tree, shadows and highlights on the trees, stalks in front of rocks.

To make a tree trunk, begin at the bottom and straight-stitch from root to a main branch. Proceed back down and come up again, this time creating another main branch. Return to the base of the trunk again, up to the first main branch, and out to a smaller limb. Continue in this way, always returning to the trunk to thicken it, and then back out to the terminal branches. End where you began. To make leaves on the tree, use a fine straight stitch and work in tight little circles. For rivers or pools of

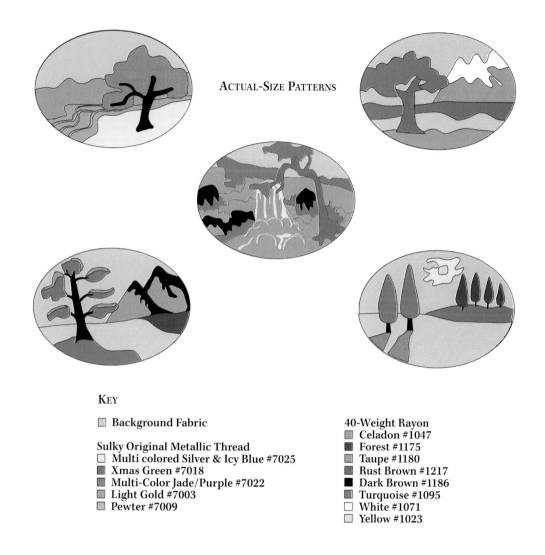

ACTUAL-SIZE PATTERNS

KEY

☐ Background Fabric

Sulky Original Metallic Thread
☐ Multi colored Silver & Icy Blue #7025
■ Xmas Green #7018
▨ Multi-Color Jade/Purple #7022
▨ Light Gold #7003
▨ Pewter #7009

40-Weight Rayon
▨ Celadon #1047
■ Forest #1175
▨ Taupe #1180
▨ Rust Brown #1217
■ Dark Brown #1186
▨ Turquoise #1095
☐ White #1071
☐ Yellow #1023

water, work in gentle curves. For waterfall, use straight, vertical lines, with tight little circles for bubbles and foam at the bottom. Use silver thread to highlight the water.

Mounting: Cut away all long thread ends on back of work. Cut out slightly beyond oval outline. Carefully tear away backing. Place the clear plastic window from the box lid over the stitched design, and trim stitchery to the same size all around. Also use this window to cut out an extra layer of thin batting.

Following manufacturer's instructions, insert stitchery (do not use the plastic window), batting provided, and extra batting into the frame, then push in the metal back until it snaps into place. Use rubber cement to glue the velveteen oval over the metal backing.

Optional Box Embellishment: Use markers to add simple dots, lines or geometric patterns all around the sides of the porcelain box. Refer to the photo for suggestions. ✧

TWIG CHAIR AND LOVESEAT

Dimensions: Chair, 3″ wide by 2″ deep by 5³⁄₈″ high; Loveseat, 4¹⁄₂″ wide by 2″ deep by 5³⁄₈″ high

Materials & Tools

- 3″ grapevine wreath
- Twigs, about ¹⁄₄″ wide
- A few dried mini rosebuds
- 1 package (4 stems, each with 3 leaves) of 2″ velvet rose leaves
- Bucket
- Scrap wood (a 6″ length of 1 x 4 is sufficient)
- Hammer
- Nails
- Clippers or small saw
- Mini hot glue gun and glue stick

Directions

CHAIR

Preparation: Clip away the wrappings on the grapevine wreath and soak it in a water-filled bucket overnight or until vine is pliable and easy to work with.

Making the Heart Back: Trace the actual-size heart pattern and tape onto a board. Hammer nails into the board, evenly spaced around the pattern and approximately ³⁄₈″ apart. Starting at the V, or

bottom of the heart, wind the grapevine around the outside of the heart 2 or 3 times. Then begin crisscrossing and free-form weaving the vine across the pattern to create a lattice. Finish off each heart by overcasting all around the outer edges, gathering and incorporating any loose vines. Tuck the vine end into the overcast strands. Allow the piece to dry partially, then remove it carefully from the nails. Let the piece dry completely.

Making the Seat: Mark a 2¹⁄₂″ x 2″ rectangle on paper, then tape this pattern onto the board. Hammer nails into board all around the pattern, evenly spaced and approximately ³⁄₈″ apart. Wind grapevine around the outside of the rectangle 2 or 3 times. Then begin crisscrossing and free-form weaving the vine across the pattern to create the seat. Overcast the edges, tuck in the ends, let dry partially, and remove from nails as before.

Assembly: Using a saw or clippers, cut five 2″ lengths and two 1¹⁄₂″ lengths from twigs. Set one 2″ length into each of the four corners of the chair seat for chair legs. Hot-glue in place. For braces, glue the remaining 2″ twig length to the underseat of the chair, across the back of the front chair legs; glue the shorter pieces to the underseat, starting from the 2″ brace and butting up against the back legs. These twigs will protrude about ¹⁄₂″ beyond the back of the seat to support the heart chair back. Hot-glue the bottom of the heart-shaped chair back to the back edge of the chair seat, securing it

ACTUAL-SIZE PATTERN
FOR HEART BACK

between the twig braces. Finish off by gluing two 2½" pieces of straight grapevine pieces across the front of the seat for an apron (this hides dabs of hot glue).

LOVESEAT

Weaving: Create 2 heart backs, following the directions above. As you overcast the edges of the second heart, overlap the side of the first heart and catch that in the wrappings. Referring to the directions for the chair seat above, create a 4" x 2" seat.

Assembly: Cut four 2" lengths and two 1¾" lengths from twigs, using clippers or a saw. Set a 2" leg into each corner of the seat and hot-glue in place. Glue a 1¾" twig between front and back legs on each side for a brace. Glue heart chair backs to rear edge of seat, propping the assembly against something as glue sets. Create armrests from 6" pieces of curved grapevine, and hot-glue along front legs with ends at heart back. Finish off loveseat by gluing two straight grapevine pieces across the front of seat as an apron, to hide the glue.

Floral Embellishments: Separate the leaves from one stem of velvet leaves. Trim stems from 4 rosebuds. Wrap the leaf stems over the back or around the leg of furniture as shown, or use them to cover any hot glue that is still visible. Hot-glue none, one or three rosebuds to the base of the leaves. ◊

STENCILED BOXES

Dimensions: Heart-Shaped Box, 3¼" by 3¼" by 1½" high; Round Box, 2½" in diameter and 1¾" high

Materials & Tools

- ❧ *Unfinished lidded containers: papier mâché heart shaped box and/or round wooden box, dimensions as suggested in specifications above*

- ❧ *American Traditional Stencils*: GS-137 Spring Heart for heart-shaped box; MS-96 Heart Trim Stencil, BL-121 Heart & Ribbon Stencil, and BL-134 Doodle Stencil*
- ❧ *Acrylic paint: white, light blue, pink, metallic gold*
- ❧ *Oil sticks*: Yellow, red, blue, green*
- ❧ *Quick-drying white craft glue*
- ❧ *Prisma glitter**
- ❧ *Acrylic sealer (optional)*
- ❧ *6" plastic foam plate, for palette*
- ❧ *Small sea sponge*
- ❧ *Masking tape*
- ❧ *¼" stencil brushes*
- ❧ *½" flat paintbrush*
- ❧ *Liner brush*

*Available from American Traditional Stencils

Directions

Preparation: Read the "Stenciling Know-How," on page 50. Use the ½" flat paintbrush and white acrylic paint to basecoat the box and lid, inside and out, on all surfaces. Let the box and lid dry on a wax paper or cellophane-covered surface.

Sponging: Squeeze a ¾" circle of pink or blue paint in the center of a disposable palette. Mix in a little white paint to create a pale pastel shade. Moisten the sponge with water, dip it into the paint, and tap lightly around the outside surfaces of the box and lid. For the heart box, light pink was used. For the round box, light blue was sponged, allowed to dry, and then light pink was lightly sponged on top of that.

Stenciling: Place stencils first on the center of the lid, then along the sides of the box; following the individual directions below. Tape the stencil

Use masking tape to secure the stencil in place on the object or surface you are stenciling. Squeeze or spoon a teaspoon of the desired acrylic paint onto a palette, such as a plastic margarine tub or lid. If you are using oil sticks or stencil creams, use a paper towel to wipe off the layer of "skin" that forms on the outside, and rub some of the moist substance onto the palette. Dab the end of a dry brush lightly into the paint or pigment. Swirl the bristles onto a paper towel to remove excess paint—in fact, dab most of the paint off the brush. There should be very little paint left on the brush. Pounce brush with an up-and-down motion over the stencil openings. Remove the stencil and wipe it clean with a dry rag or a damp paper towel.

When using more than one color for a stencil motif, start with the lightest color and work to the darkest color. Don't be afraid to overlap colors; this adds depth and sophistication to the finished effect. Pigments from the oil sticks (or stencil creams) stay moist and are easy to blend on the palette, or as you are stenciling on smooth surfaces.

Use a clean brush for each color of paint to avoid a "muddying" of colors. Rinse the acrylic paint from a brush before it dries and hardens the bristles. You can clean brushes dipped in oil stick or stencil creams using water, but a simple dry rag will usually wipe them clean. Before returning to stenciling, be sure to remove all of the moisture from a freshly washed brush by rubbing the bristles on an old terry towel.

Mask out the portions of the stencil you are not using with masking tape. This allows you to fit in motifs as desired. Use the reverse side of a stencil to create mirror images. Use a liner brush dipped in the same or contrasting colors to correct or embellish motifs.

STENCILED BOXES
continued

in place. Referring to the photograph for suggested colors, stencil with pigment from the oil sticks.

For the heart-shaped box, stencil GS-137 centered on the lid. With the lid in place for optimal positioning, stencil the heart and swirl pattern along the sides of the box bottom, repeating the motif at evenly spaced intervals all around.

For the round box, stencil MS-96 on the top of the lid. Let that dry, and then make a lacy edge around the top of the lid using BL-121 as follows: Position three scallops toward the edge of the lid. Use a stencil brush with white paint and dry-brush off the edge. Repeat until the scallops form a complete circle. Use the heart motif from BL-134 and red paint to add a tiny heart at each scallop around the lid. Stencil around the sides of the box bottom, repeating the corner motif from BL-121 (an $1/8''$ heart with folk art strokes) at four evenly-spaced intervals.

Embellishments: For the heart-shaped box, apply light blue acrylic paint with an almost dry brush along the sides of the lid, slightly past the edges onto the top of the lid, and along the box's bottom edges. Use a liner brush and gold acrylic paint to add veins to the leaves, to accentuate the flower centers, and to "antique" the hard edges of the box. Use a clean liner brush to apply glue around the edges of the stenciled heart. Sprinkle with glitter, then shake off excess. For the round box, apply dots of glue and glitter to each tiny heart around the top of the lid. This box has a ridge along the bottom that received a coat of white paint to match the edges of the lid.

Finishing: If desired, spray with two light coats of acrylic sealer. ✦

ROUND CRYSTAL BOX

shown on page 36

Dimensions: Lid, 1½" in diameter; box 1⅞" in diameter at the bottom, 1⅜" high

Materials & Tools

- ❧ *Framecraft small round crystal box CT1, from Mill Hill*
- ❧ *Small piece of confederate gray Belfast linen, 32-count, from Zweigart*
- ❧ *1 skein of blue-gray, six-strand embroidery floss: DMC #926 or Coats & Clark's Anchor #850*
- ❧ *1 package Champagne Petite Glass Seed Bead #42027, from Mill Hill*
- ❧ *Small piece of thin batting*
- ❧ *Embroidery and beading needles*

Directions

Preparation: Read "How to Cross Stitch," on page 125.

Embroidery: Use one strand of floss in an embroidery needle. Following the chart, refer to the stitch detail and key, and work smyrna crosses over 4 threads of the linen. Start with a traditional cross stitch, making two diagonal stitches. On top of each large cross stitch, make a vertical and then a horizontal stitch. To make smyrna crosses uniform looking, stitches must consistently follow the same order and the same direction.

Beadwork: Use a beading needle and one strand of floss to sew on beads. Beads are in clusters of four, with the bead positioned on the diagonal, so that each cluster resembles a tiny diamond shape. Take care in following the chart, stitching on the beads with a half cross stitch that goes in the appropriate direction.

Mounting: Place the clear plastic window from the box lid over the back of the stitched design, and trim stitchery to the same size all around. Also use this window to cut out an extra layer of thin batting. Following manufacturer's instructions, insert stitchery (do not use the plastic window), batting provided, and extra batting into the frame, then push in the metal back until it snaps into place. Use rubber cement to glue the velveteen circle over the metal backing. ❧

CHART FOR ROUND CRYSTAL BOX

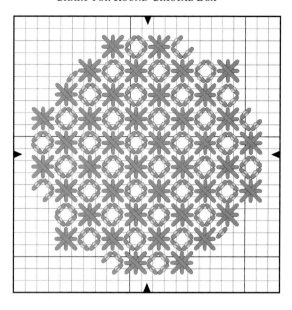

KEY

 Smyrna cross over 4 threads

Bead stitched with a half cross stitch going from lower left to upper right

Bead stitched with a half cross stitch going from lower right to upper left

SMYRNA CROSS STITCH

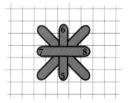

51

"Gift" Box

shown on page 36

Dimensions: $2^3/_4''$ by $2''$ by $1^1/_4''$ high

Materials & Tools

- Fimo Modeling Material* in fir green pink, and white
- Gold Metallic Powder*
- Matte Varnish*
- Optional: Roses Push Molds*
- Small rectangular cardboard jewelry box with lid
- Pink seed bead
- Craft knife; ruler; cutting mat; rolling pin

    *From AMACO

Directions

Covering the Box: Read and refer to "Working with Polymer Clay" on page 18. Create a marbleized surface by cutting up 1 part white clay to 3 parts green clay. Roll all of the chunks in a ball. Roll the ball into a coil, double it over, and twist it to obtain undulating striations. Roll out a thin sheet of marbled clay $^1/_8''$ thick. Place the box lid and bottom on clay and use a craft knife to cut a rectangle to correspond to each of these surfaces. Place the lid on the box and measure the height of the box sides that are not covered by the lid. Measure the circumference of the box. Cut a strip to wrap around the sides of the box below the lid, and another to wrap around the sides of the lid. Press each of these shapes lightly over their corresponding surfaces, and rub the joints to seal them, leaving slightly rounded edges.

Making the Gift Ribbon: Roll out the white clay into a $^1/_8''$ thick sheet. Cut $^1/_4''$ wide strips. Rub gold metallic powder on the top surface and the edges of the strips. Lay two intersecting strips across the lid, trimming the ends even with the edge of the lid. Use another strip for a bow, simply making two loops and leaving two streamer ends; cut the ends on an angle. Arrange the bow at the intersection of the first two strips.

Making a Rose: Use pink clay to make a rose, fir green clay to make two leaves: Use molds or make them yourself as follows: For a rose, start with six $^1/_8''$ balls, and four $^1/_4''$ balls. Flatten all but one $^1/_8''$ ball (reserve this for the flower center) with your pinky. Wrap the flower center with the smaller pieces, attaching them at the bottom of the ball, and staggering the placements so they overlap each other and surround the center. Curl the top edges out. End with the larger flattened pieces. For leaves, use a craft knife to cut a football-shaped piece $^1/_2''$ long, and to carve veins onto the surface. Place a leaf on either side of the rose, and place on top of the bow. Press a seed bead into the center of the rose.

Finishing: Bake the box with the lid and box bottom separated. When cool, apply a light coat of varnish to the marbleized surfaces only.

Valentine Sachets

shown on page 37

Dimensions: $2^1/_2''$ by $2^3/_4''$

Materials & Tools

- DMC Rayon Floss, one skein each color listed in the key
- Zweigart Luguna even-weave, cotton-rayon fabric, 25-count; small amount of white #100 and/or soft green #618
- Mill Hill Petite Glass Beads, 1 package each listed in the key
- Medium rickrack, $^3/_8$ yard for each
- Red satin ribbon: $^1/_8''$ wide, $^1/_4$ yard for each
- Sewing thread to match beads, rickrack, and ribbon
- Thin, fusible interfacing
- Small amount of red mini-print cotton fabric, for backing
- White small grain rice or ground potpourri
- Embroidery, beading and sewing needles
- Embroidery hoop
- Iron
- Tracing paper and pencil

- ❀ *Sewing machine*
- ❀ *Funnel*
- ❀ *Optional: magnifier*

Directions

Preparation: Read "How to Cross Stitch" on page 125.

Stitching: Cross stitch using 1 strand of floss and working over 2 threads. Follow the chart and key, but notice that you may use pink or red for the dotted background on the rose design. Backstitch where indicated, using 1 strand of floss as well. For the green sachet, make lazy-daisy stitch leaves, referring to the embroidery stitch detail on page 124.

Beadwork (green sachet only): Use a beading needle and sew on each bead separately with one strand of white sewing thread. Begin with the red beads, referring to the chart for position, and surround each with 6 pearly white beads. Add a few single white beads in scattered positions as suggested on the chart.

Assembly: Fuse interfacing to the back of the cross stitch. Trace the actual-size heart pattern on page 48 onto tracing paper, and center it carefully over the cross stitch. Pin in place, and cut out ¼" beyond the pattern all around, for seam allowances.

Starting and ending at the bottom point of heart, pin rickrack around the edges of the cross-stitched heart on the right side. Using a contrast-color thread, hand-baste through the center of the rickrack. For a hanging loop, cut a 4" length of satin ribbon. Fold it in half, and pin it to the front of the heart with the loop at the center and the cut ends at the center top, even with the raw edges. Place the cross-stitched front on fabric for backing, with right sides facing. Machine-stitch along basting stitches, leaving a 1½" opening along one side. Cut the backing to the same size as the front. Cut across the bottom point, as close to the stitching as possible. Clip up to the stitches at the center top and along the curves.

Turn the sachet to the right side. Use a pin to pull out the bottom point. Finger-press the seams. Use a funnel to fill the sachet with rice or potpourri. Turn in the open edges and slip-stitch closed by hand. Use 5" of satin ribbon to tie a tiny bow. Tack it to the base of the hanging loop. ❧

CHARTS FOR VALENTINE SACHETS

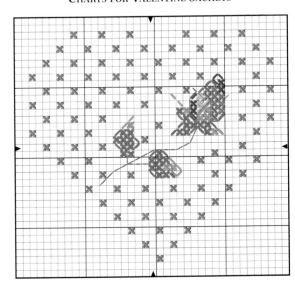

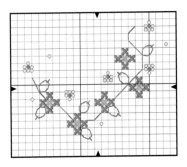

KEY

DMC Rayon Floss
Cross Stitch and Half Cross Stitch
- ✖ Pink #33689
- ✖ Red #30349
- ✖ Rose #33350
- ✖ Green #30700
- ✖ Mint Green #30955
- ✖ Yellow #30744
- — Backstitch with Green #30700
- ◠ Lazy daisy stitch with Green #30700

Beadwork with Mill Hill Petite Glass Beads
- ● Red #42013
- ○ White #40479

Chapter Three

Traditions

❖

Miniature toys and animals, splendid baubles and tassels were among the abundant ornaments used when Queen Victoria and Prince Albert first brought the Yuletide tree-trimming custom to England during the mid-nineteenth century.

Ritual can magnify the smallest symbol of faith and worship. My husband's family always decorates at least one little Christmas tree in addition to the grand,  ceiling-high one. Creating and displaying Judaica is one of the ways I celebrate my religious heritage. The custom of decorating for the holidays or the holy days is for many a nostalgic connection to years of family tradition and centuries of exuberant celebration; it is also an eloquent link to the future.

Traditions

PREVIOUS PAGE:

Wreathed in Glory

Bonita Salamanca used DMC embroidery floss for the Della Robbia and grapevine motifs, punctuating her cross stitches with glass seed beads on a half cross stitch. They're perfectly scaled for a tree ornament, but hung in a window, they're dazzling. Light comes through the perforations in the vinyl backing, the glass seed beads and the sheer ribbon.

Crafted for Christmas

These tiny ornaments trim a topiary tree, but consider them also for package decorations, party favors, napkin ring decorations, three-dimensional season's greetings, baubles to dangle from an earring or other jewelry finding. In the dollhouse, a square sachet may be used as a pillow; a beaded ball may become a Victorian chandelier. Take your pick of six different patterns for the crocheted Christmas ball, five different patterns for the cross-stitch sachet ornaments, three variations of the beaded balls, and as many elegant tassel designs as colors you fancy.

In Detail

Here's a closer look at the ornaments arrayed on the page before:

For each of the beaded balls at far left and tassels at far right, Kathleen George covered a tiny ball of Styrofoam. The balls are coiled with strings of pearls or beaded chain; ribbon roses and tear-drop pearls or crystal prisms embellish the north and south poles. The tassels showcase gleaming metallic threads; passementerie, pearls and scalloping swags of seed beads hug the neck of each tassel like a jeweled choker.

The secret to the crocheted Christmas balls below is an openwork pouch with a drawstring to snugly encase a bright silk mini-ball. Each one features a different design. They were made by Bonita Salamanca using DMC's ecru Cebelia #30.

Penny Kimball cross-stitched with rayon and metallic threads from DMC to create the linen pillows, opposite. Seed beads accent each design. Use a fragrant balsam potpourri to stuff them. Set them in lingerie drawers for sachets, or catch the little loops of the twisted cord on the hooks of clothes hangers for pomanders.

Emblazoned with Pride

This mezuzah case is a strikingly beautiful ceremonial piece. It contains the passages from Deuteronomy 6:4-9 and 11:13-21, glorifying God and obligating the Jew to inscribe the words "on the doorposts of thy house." Jane "Shana" Blum gilded the Zweigart needlepoint canvas and left the background unworked. For the character (the first letter of the Hebrew word for Almighty) she used flamestitch, alluding to the burning bush or the eternal light, symbols of God's presence and infinite power.

Here, O Israel

Hanukkah menorah by Kathleen George features a miniature rendition of ancient Jerusalem, with ceramic pots along the walls of the city to hold birthday candles. Granitex modeling compound has a pinkish, stone-like texture, which Kathleen burnished with a little gold powder. A symbol most commonly associated with Judaism and the graphic used on the Israeli flag is the six-pointed star of David.
Linda Driscoll used metallic threads from DMC to crochet the two intertwined triangles and to braid the long tail for use as a bookmark.

Traditions

Ceremonial Vestments

Breastplates and bottle stoppers enhance wine flasks for ritual splendor. Every Sabbath, as well as on other holy days and festivals, Jews chant a prayer of thanksgiving over a cup of wine. As the ceremonies at home elevate wine to a special place, I put the wine into decorative bottles and dressed them in holiday finery. Shrink art plastic, rubber-stamped to frame a little Hebrew (far left, the word Passover; far right, "To Life!"), French (Le Vin means "the Wine"), or English label, comes down to 40 percent of its original size as it bakes. Simultaneously, any mistakes shrink to negligible proportions. These pieces acquire the look of porcelain, nickel-thick. Also baked in the oven, the crowning glories secured to bottle corks are sculptures of modeling compound, studded with glass beads.

63

each bead on a half cross stitch. Work all these half cross stitches from lower left to upper right, so that all beads appear uniform.

Assembly: Cut out the motif one row of plastic canvas beyond the stitching. Cut 10″ of ribbon for a hanging loop. Wrap it around the wreath and tie a knot 1″ from the ends. Use the remaining ribbon to tie a simple bow, with loops 1½″ to 2″ in length. Hot-glue the knot of the bow to the wreath at a point opposite the hanging loop. Hot-glue the stitched motif to the wreath so it overlaps the hanging loop or the bow. Cut notches into the ribbon ends, or fringe them: Cut away the wire and selvage for ⅜″, and use the point of a needle to pull out crosswise threads.

BEADED WREATHS

Dimensions: 9″ long from top of ribbon hanger to bottom of streamer; Della Robbia motif, 2¼″ by 2⅜″; Grape motif, 1¾″ by 3″

Materials:

- ⚜ *DMC Six-Strand Embroidery Floss, 1 skein each color listed in the key*
- ⚜ *Mill Hill Seed Beads, 1 package each color listed in the key*
- ⚜ *White Nymo beading thread, available from Mill Hill*
- ⚜ *Ecru plastic canvas, 14-count, from Darice*
- ⚜ *3″ grapevine wreath*
- ⚜ *Embroidery needle; beading needle size 10 or 13*
- ⚜ *Small, sharp scissors*
- ⚜ *Hot glue gun and glue stick*

Directions:

Stitching: Read "How to Cross Stitch" on page 125. Following the chart and key, make cross stitches for all symbols that represent floss. Use an embroidery needle and 3 strands of floss. For the Della Robbia, make pine needles with backstitch stems and long-stitch needles.

Beadwork: Follow the chart and key to add beads. Use a beading needle and beading thread, and apply

CHART FOR GRAPE WREATH

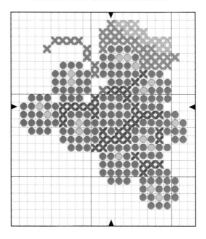

KEY

DMC Six-Strand Embroidery Floss
Crss Stitch

- ✖ Medium Green #367
- ✖ Light Green #3817
- ✖ Deep Rose #3688
- ✖ Brown #829

Beadwork with Mill Hill Glass Seed Beads

- ● Iris #00252
- ● Coral #00275

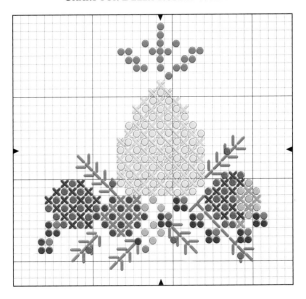

KEY

DMC Six-Strand Embroidery Floss
Cross Stitch
✖ Red #349
✖ Deep Rose #3688
✖ Light Green #3817
✖ Medium Green #367
✖ Light Violet #210
✖ Violet #208
✖ Yellow Gold #726

🖊 Backstitch stems and long-stitch
  needles with Medium Green #367

Beadwork with Mill Hill Seed Beads
● Christmas Red #00165
○ Dusty Rose #02005
○ Yellow #00128
● Emerald #00332
○ Christmas Green #00167
● Violet #00206
● Iris #00252

SACHET ORNAMENTS

Dimensions: Approximately 2¹/₂″ square

Materials & Tools

- *DMC Rayon Floss, 1 skein each color listed in the key*
- *DMC Gold 6-Strand Metallic Floss*
- *Zweigart Antique Ivory Cashel linen, 28-count*
- *Mill Hill Petite Glass Beads, 1 package each color listed in the key*
- *Sewing thread: ecru, and colors to match the rayon floss used for the trim*
- *Thin, fusible interfacing*
- *Small amount of satin fabric, for backing*
- *Balsam potpourri (see recipe on page 67)*
- *Embroidery, beading and sewing needles*
- *Embroidery hoop*
- *Iron*
- *Tracing paper and pencil*
- *Sewing machine*
- *Funnel*
- *Optional: Magnifier; Spinster from Viking Husqvarna & White, for making twisted cord trim*

SACHET ORNAMENTS

continued

Directions

Preparation: Read "How to Cross Stitch" on page 125 and prepare the fabric.

Stitching: Cross-stitch using 1 strand of floss, working over 2 threads. Follow the appropriate chart and key. Backstitch where indicated, using 1 strand of floss here as well.

Beadwork: Use a beading needle and sew on each bead separately with one strand of ecru sewing thread. For the utmost in durability, pass through each bead twice. For lines of beads, such as the angel's halo, string on all the beads, then take a stitch to anchor the thread between beads, couching them into position.

Assembly: Mark a 2½″ square on tracing paper, and cut it out. Center this pattern carefully over the cross stitch design, lining up the edges with the grain of the fabric. Pin in place, and cut out ¼″ beyond pattern all around, for seam allowances. Cut a same-size piece from fabric for the back.

Pin front to back, with right sides facing. Machine-stitch around, ¼″ from raw edges, and leaving a 1 ½″ opening along the center of one side. Clip across the seam allowance at each corner, as close to the stitching as possible. Turn the piece to the right side. Use a pin to pull out the corners. Finger-press the seams. Use a funnel to fill the interior with potpourri. (Use the recipe opposite, if desired.) Fill sachets to desired plumpness. These ornaments are lightly filled, so that the surfaces remain flat and the designs are completely visible. For more firmly stuffed ornaments, use a crochet hook or bluntly pointed object to push the

SNOWFLAKE

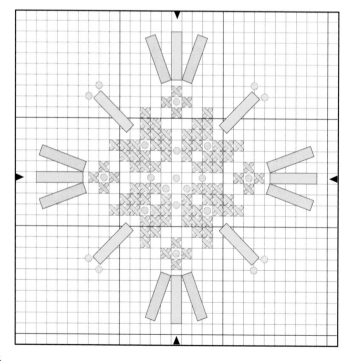

KEY

DMC Metallic Floss
Cross Stitch and Half Cross Stitch
Gold #5282
Silver #5283

Beadwork with Mill Hill Beads
Ice Petite Glass Seed Bead #42010
Small Ice Bugle Bead #72010
Small Victorian Gold Bugle
Bead #72011

Twisted Cord:
Gold and Silver Metallic Floss

potpourri into the corners. Turn in the open edges and slip-stitch the ornament closed by hand.

Trimming: Cut 2½ yards of six-strand rayon floss in one of the accent colors used in the cross-stitch design. Cut the same length from gold floss and knot together at one end. Make a twisted cord: Use the Spinster, and follow the instructions for making rope. Or, use a partner to twist the strands together while you hold the strands out taut, tie the strands at each end onto the center of a pencil. Twist the pencils in opposite directions—just until the floss starts to kink. Keeping the twisted strands stretched out, grab the center, and slide a hand toward the ends, allowing the two halves to twist together. Tie a knot to secure the ends. Using ecru sewing thread, slip-stitch the twisted cord along the seams of the sachets, forming a loop and leaving 2″ ends at one corner (top). You may knot the ends ¼″ from the corner and trim the ends to ¼″ beyond the knot, or you may unravel the threads beyond the loop, for fringe. ☙

Recipe for Balsam Potpourri

Select the new growth of balsam needles at the ends of branches. Strip the branch of its needles, and place the needles on a window screen in a dry place, such as an attic. Prop up the screen on blocks or jars, so that air can circulate under the needles as well as over them. Leave this setup for at least a week, longer if the air is damp. Pour the needles into jars, adding one tablespoon of salt for every ½ cup of needles. Allow this mixture to cure for about 3 weeks, shaking the jar once or twice weekly. When the needles are thoroughly dry, crush the mixture using a mini food processor or a mortar and pestle.

FRENCH HORN & POINSETTIAS

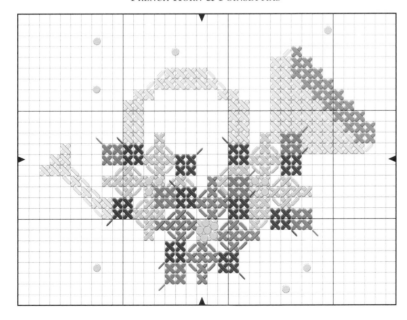

KEY

DMC Rayon Floss, unless otherwise indicated

Cross Stitch and Half Cross Stitch

- ✖ Ultra Dark Dusty Rose #33350
- ✖ Bright Christmas Green #30700
- ✖ Dark Coral #30349
- ✖ Light Topaz #30726
- ✖ Medium Rose #30899
- ✖ Medium Golden Brown #30976
- ✖ Gold Metallic Floss #5282

Beadwork with Mill Hill Petite Glass Beads
- ● Victorian Gold #42011

Twisted Cord:
Red Rayon Floss #30349 and
Gold Metallic Floss #5282

CAROUSEL PONY

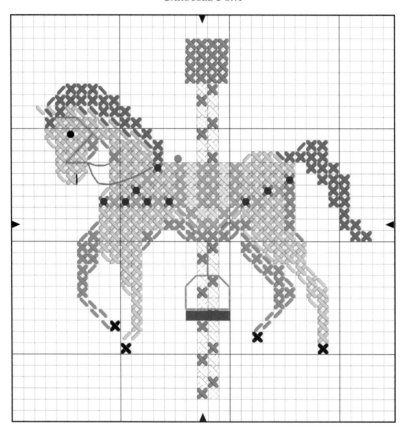

KEY

DMC Rayon Floss, unless otherwise indicated
Cross Stitch and Half Cross Stitch
✘ Black #30310
⬩ Snow White #35200
✘ Medium Golden Brown #30976
✘ Medium Nile Green #30913
✘ Geranium #30956
✘ Very Dark Mahogany #30300
✘ Light Old Gold #30676
⬩ Gold Metallic Floss #5282

Backstitch
— Medium Golden Brown #30976
— Geranium #30956 (let the reins hang loosely)

Beadwork with Mill Hill Beads
● Black Seed Bead #02014 (pony's eye)
▬ Root Beer Medium Bugle Bead #82023
● Red Red Glass Seed Bead #02013
● Red Red Petite Glass Seed Bead #42013

Twisted Cord: Red Rayon Floss #30956 and Gold
Metallic Floss #5282

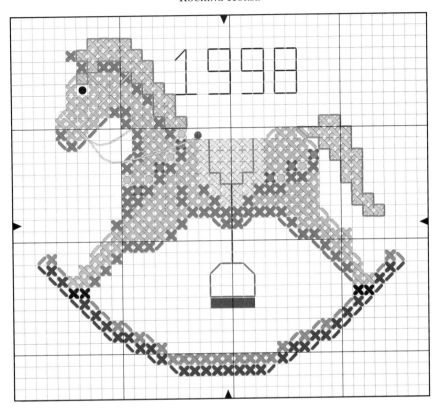

KEY

DMC Rayon Floss, unless
otherwise indicated
Cross Stitch and Half Cross Stitch

- ✖ Medium Seagreen #30959
- ✖ Light Seagreen #30964
- ✖ Light Old Gold #30676
- ✖ Light Violet #30554
- ✖ Medium Golden Brown #30976
- ✖ Very Dark Mahogany #30300
- ✖ Black #30310
- ✖ Gold Metallic Floss #5282

Backstitch

- — Gold Metallic Floss #5282 (let the
  reins hang loosely)
- — Light Violet #30554
- — Medium Golden Brown #30976
- — Black #30310

Beadwork with Mill Hill Beads

- ● Old Rose Petite Glass Seed Bead #40553
- ○ Victorian Gold Petite Glass Seed Bead #42011
- ● Old Rose Glass Seed Bead #00553
- ▬ Root Beer Medium Bugle Bead #82023
- ● Black Seed Bead #02014 (horse's eye)

Twisted Cord: Light Violet Rayon Floss #30554
and Gold Metallic Floss #5282

ANGEL

KEY

DMC Rayon Floss, unless
otherwise indicated
Cross Stitch and Half Cross Stitch
❌ Medium Golden Brown #30976
✕ Snow White #35200
✕ Off White #30746
❌ Medium Nile Green #30913
❌ Kelly Green #30702
✕ Geranium #30956
❌ Medium Rose #30899
✕ Light Coral #30352
✕ Gold Metallic Floss #5282

Twisted Cord: Kelly Green Rayon Floss #30702
and Gold Metallic Floss #5282

Backstitch
— Gold Metallic
  Floss #5282
— Very Dark
  Mahogany #30300
— Kelly Green #30702
— Black #30310

**Beadwork with Mill
Hill Petite Glass Beads
Victorian Gold**
⬤ #42011

BEADED BALLS

Dimensions: $1\frac{1}{4}''$ in diameter, $2\frac{1}{4}''$ long, not
including hanging loop

Materials & Tools (for each)

- Styrofoam brand plastic foam ball, $1''$ in
  diameter
- Peel 'n Stick adhesive
- $2\frac{1}{2}''$ yards of Facets Thread, by Kreinik or 1 yard
  of strung pearl trim or 1 yard of ball chain
- $\frac{1}{2}''$ craft pin
- Gold eye pin
- Gold jump ring
- Gold metallic thread for hanging loop
- Scraps of optional trimmings: $\frac{1}{4}''$ metallic or satin
  braid, guimpe, or fancy trim; $\frac{1}{8}''$ wide satin or
  metallic ribbon; small ribbon roses or ribbon
  flowers; seed beads
- $1''$ teardrop crystal or $\frac{1}{2}''$ teardrop pearl
- Wood skewer
- Sewing and beading needles
- Mini hot glue gun and glue stick
- Jewelry pliers

Directions

Covering the Ball: Pierce the foam ball with the pointed end of a skewer. Anchor the opposite end of the skewer in a large piece of foam, a weighted vase, or between your knees. Cover the entire surface of the foam ball with small pieces of adhesive. Mentally visualize where the skewer pierces the ball as the south pole, and the center as an equator. Beginning at the equator, wind bead trim or fancy thread around the ball until you reach the north pole. Cut the strand, then begin again at the equator and cover the lower hemisphere of the ball in the same way. Remove the skewer when you get to the south pole, and cover it. Roll the ball gently in your hand to ensure that the beads or fancy thread have adhered securely.

Embellishing: Use dots of hot glue and craft pins to attach a fancy trim around the equator of the ball. If you wish, sew loops of seed beads to the trim. Accent the tops of each scallop with a contrast-color seed bead. Use an eye pin to attach a drop pearl or a crystal at the south pole of the ball. Glue a 1/8" ribbon bow and/or a ribbon flower to the north pole.

Finishing: Stitch gold metallic thread through the embellishment at the north pole. Bring the thread ends together and knot, for a hanging loop as long or short as your needs dictate. Trim the excess thread beyond the knot. ◊

- *Fine gold metallic thread*
- *Mill Hill seed beads in an iridescent or opalescent tone*
- *6 crystal barrel beads, 6mm long*
- *Scrap of metallic trim, braid or guimpe, 1/4" to 1/2" wide*
- *1/2" bell cap jewelry finding*
- *Tacky craft glue*
- *Corrugated cardboard, 2" x 4" rectangle*
- *Very sharp scissors*
- *Iron*
- *Beading needle*

Directions

Reduce the Ball: Roll the foam ball gently on work surface until the ball is a smooth, even 3/4" in diameter.

Make the Tassel: Cut an 8" length from both spools of braid, and set aside. Wrap the rest of the spools of braid around a stiff piece of 4" cardboard. Using steam and a press cloth, iron the thread while it is still wrapped around the cardboard to remove any creases. Insert one of the 8" reserved pieces of braid under the wrappings and center it at one 2" edge of the cardboard. Use this strand to tie the wrapped thread together tightly. At the opposite edge of the cardboard, slip scissors under the loops and cut across, releasing the braid from the cardboard. See figure 1 on page 72.

Center the tied braid over the foam ball. Spread the threads out to cover the entire ball and then

TASSEL ORNAMENTS

Dimensions: About 3" long, not including the hanging loop

Materials & Tools (for each)

- *Styrofoam brand plastic foam ball, 1" in diameter*
- *2 spools of Kreinik Metallic Very Fine Braid #4, in the color of your choice*
- *Black beading thread*

TASSEL ORNAMENTS
continued

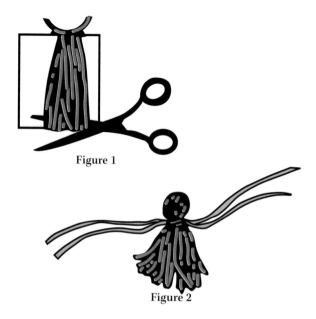

Figure 1

bring them together at the base of the ball. Use a double strand of gold thread to wrap around the strands, forming a "neck." See figure 2. Continue wrapping tightly to widen the neck to about $\frac{1}{8}''$ thick and $\frac{1}{4}''$ wide, then tie off, leaving the thread ends very long. Keeping these out of the way, hold all the braid threads between your first and second fingers and trim the ends even, using a sharp pair of scissors.

Embellishing: With the gold thread ends still out of the way, glue a $1\frac{1}{2}''$ piece of fancy metallic trim over the neck of the tassel. Now, thread one of the strands of gold thread onto a beading needle. To facilitate this, put a tiny amount of glue on the end of the thread and let it dry. This will make the hairy end of the metallic thread easier to thread through the tiny eye of the beading needle. String loops of seed beads from the trim. These tassels each have approximately 5 loops of 21 seed beads per loop. Also stitch the crystal barrel beads around the wrapped neck of the tassel. Use the other strands of gold thread as necessary. When this is done, weave under any remaining gold thread and trim away excess.

Figure 2

Finishing: For a hanging loop, thread a 6″ length of gold metallic thread under the braid at the very top of the tassel; bring the gold thread ends together and knot. Open a bell cap to fit the top of the tassel, thread the hanging loop through the hole in the top, and attach to the top of the tassel with glue. ◊

Crochet Abbreviations

ch	–	chain stitch
dc	–	double crochet
hdc	–	half double crochet
sc	–	single crochet
sk	–	skip
sl st	–	slip stitch
st	–	stitch
tr	–	triple crochet
dtr	–	double triple crochet
*	–	repeat directions following * as indicated

CROCHET CHRISTMAS BALLS

Dimensions: 1″ in diameter

Materials & Tools

- 1 ball of DMC Cebelia Crochet Cotton size 30 in ivory
- Red satin balls, 25mm
- Sheer red ribbon with gold edging: ½″ wide, 6″ length per ornament
- Crochet hook, size 10

FIVE–PETAL DAISY

Round 1: Ch 8, sc in first ch to form a ring, * ch 7, sc in same ch,* repeat from * to * 2 times, ch 3, tr in same ch, ch 1, sc in same space.

Round 2: Ch 6, * sc in ch-7 loop,* repeat from * to * 4 times, ch 3, tr in first sc, ch 1, sc in same space.

Round 3: Ch 8, * sc in ch-6 loop,* repeat from * to * 4 times; ch 3, dtr in sc.

Rounds 4 and 5: Repeat round 3. Fasten off.

Finishing: Complete same as for the Star design.

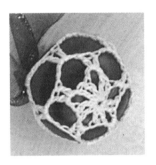

Directions

STAR

Round 1: Ch 4, 1 dc, ch 3, 2 dc in first ch. * Ch 3, 2 dc, ch 3,* repeat from * to * 3 times, 2 dc. Ch 1, hdc in third ch of beginning ch 4. (5 ch-3 spaces with 2 dc in between).

Round 2: Ch 3, dc in same space, * ch 5, 2 dc in next space,* repeat from * to * 4 times; ch 2, dc in top of first ch 3.

Round 3: Ch 3, 1 dc in same space, * ch 6, 2 dc in next ch 5,* repeat from * to * 4 times, ch 3, tr in first dc.

Round 4: Ch 3, 1 dc in same space, * ch 7, 2 dc in next ch 6,* repeat from * to * 4 times; ch 4, tr in first dc.

Finishing: Fasten off, leaving a 5″ tail of thread. Weave thread through loops of the last round. Slip cover over the silk ball; pull thread tightly at the top and fasten securely. Slip a ribbon through the ring of the ball, and tie in a bow. Cut ribbon ends on an angle.

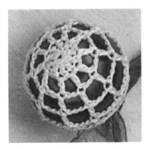

NETTING

Round 1: Ch 4, 9 dc in first ch, sl st in third st of ch 4 to form a ring.

Round 2: Ch 5, dc in first dc, * ch 2, dc in next dc,* repeat from * to * around; sl st in third ch of ch 5.

Round 3: Ch 6, dc in first dc of previous round, * ch 3, dc in next dc, * repeat from * to * around, sl st in third ch of ch 6.

Round 4: Ch 7, dc in first dc of previous round, * ch 4, dc in next dc, * repeat from * to * around, sl st in third ch of ch 7.

Round 5: Repeat round 3. Slip cover over ball.

Round 6: Repeat round 2.

Round 7: Ch 3, dc in each dc around, sl st in top of ch 3. Fasten off.

Finishing: Slip a ribbon through the ring of the ball and tie in a bow. Cut ribbon ends on an angle.

CROCHET CHRISTMAS BALLS
continued

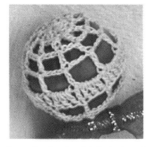

CENTER BAND

Round 1: Ch 4, 9 dc in first ch, sl st in third chain of ch 4.

Round 2: Ch 5, dc in next dc, * ch 2, dc in next dc, * repeat from * to * around. Sl st in third chain of ch 5.

Round 3: Ch 6, dc in next dc, * ch 3, dc in next dc, * repeat from * to * around. Sl st in third chain of ch 6.

Round 4: Ch 7, dc in next dc, * ch 4, dc in next dc, * repeat from * to * around. Sl st in third chain of ch 7.

Round 5: Ch 3, * 3 dc in ch-3 space, dc in next dc, * repeat from * to * around. Sl st in top of beginning ch 3.

Round 6: Ch 7, * skip 3 dc, dc in next dc, * repeat from * to * around. Sl st in third chain of ch 7.

Round 7: Repeat round 2. Slip ball into cover.

Round 8: Ch 3, dc in each dc around. Sl st in top of beginning ch 3. Fasten off.

Finishing: Complete same as for the Netting design.

IRISH ROSE

Round 1: *Ch 6, dc in first ch, ch 2,* repeat from * to * 5 times. Sl st in third ch of beginning ch 6.

Round 2: Sl st in first ch-2 space, ch 1, * sc, hdc, dc, hdc, sc* in same space, and repeat from * to * in each ch-2 space around to form 6 petals; ch 2.

Round 3: From the back, sc around the dc post of first round, ch 4, repeat around, sl in first sc.

Round 4: * Sc, hdc, 3 dc, hdc, sc, * repeat from * to * in each ch-4 space around. Sl st in first sc.

Round 5: * Ch 1, sc around post of row 4, ch 5, * repeat from * to * around, sl st in first sc.

Round 6: Sl st in ch-5 space, * sc, hdc, 5 dc, hdc, sc, * repeat from * to * in each ch-5 space around. Sl st in first sc.

Round 7: Sl st into the third dc of first petal, ch 1, sc in same dc, * ch 7, sc in third dc of next petal, * repeat from * to * 5 times; ch 3, tr in first sc of round.

Round 8: Ch 1, sc in same loop, * ch 9, sc in ch-7 loop, * repeat from * to * 5 times; ch 3, tr in first sc.

Round 9: Repeat round 8. Fasten off.

Finishing: Complete same as for the Star design.

LONG LEAVES

Round 1: Ch 4, 9 dc in first ch. Sl st in third ch of ch 4.

Round 2: Ch 3, dc in next dc, * ch 2, dc in next 2 dc, * repeat from * to * around; ch 2, sl st in top of first ch 3.

Round 3: Ch 3, dc in same st, dc in next 2 dc, ch 2, * 2 dc in next 2 dc, * repeat from * to * around, ch 2, sl st in top of first ch 3.

Round 4: Ch 3, dc in next 3 dc, ch 2, sc in ch 2 space, ch 2, * dc in next 4 dc, ch 2 sc in ch 2 space, ch 2, * repeat from * to * around. Sl st in top of ch 3.

Round 5: Ch 3, dc in next 3 dc, ch 2, sc in sc, ch 2, * dc in next 4 dc, ch 2, sc in sc, ch 2, * repeat from * to * around, sl st in top of ch 3. Slip cover over ball.

Round 6: Repeat round 5.

Round 7: Ch 3, dc in next 3 dc, ch 2, * dc in next 4 dc, ch 2,* repeat from * to * around, sl st in top of ch 3.

Round 8: Ch 3, skip next dc, ch 2 space and dc, * dc in next 2 dc, ch 2, skip 2 dc,* repeat from * to * around, sl st in top of ch 3.

Round 9: Ch 2, * hdc in ch-2 space, hdc in next 2 dc, * repeat from * to * around, sl st in top of ch 2. Fasten off.

Finishing: Complete same as for the Netting design.

Mezuzah Case

Dimensions: 1⁵/₁₆″ by 3⁹/₁₆″ by ⁵/₈″ deep

Materials & Tools

- Zweigart Mono Deluxe Canvas, 18-count, brown #1282-70, 7″ x 9″
- Kreinik Silk Serica, 1 (10m) reel each color listed in the key
- Kreinik Cable, 1 reel (10m) 002P
- Kreinik Medium Braid #16, 1 reel (10m) Gold #002
- Mill Hill Beads, 1 packet each color listed in the key
- ColorWorks Hobby Craft Quick Drying Enamel Paint .059L Metallic Brass #605
- 1 spool J. & P. Coats Dual Duty Plus Thread #309A (or the equivalent)
- Mezuzah prayer scroll, available at synagogues and Judaica shops
- #2 pencil and tracing paper
- Small, inexpensive paintbrush
- Elmer's Glue-All and small mixing cup;
- Aluminum foil
- Sharp scissors
- DMC Tapestry Needles, sizes 24, 26, 28
- Clear tape

Directions

Preparing the Canvas: Trace the actual-size pattern for the mezuzah case onto tracing paper. Cut out this pattern and center it on canvas. Make sure the long edges of the pattern are along the grain of the canvas, or running parallel and perpendicular to the canvas threads. Trace around the pattern with pencil. Place the canvas on a work surface protected with aluminum foil. Paint over the pencil lines, plus 3 strands of canvas to the inside of these lines with a mixture of one teaspoon of white glue and the same amount of water. This will keep the canvas from fraying when you finally cut out the piece. Let dry on the foil, then open any coated holes with a tapestry needle. Mix gold enamel paint thoroughly, and paint the Top, Bottom, and Front sections. Let dry on the foil for several hours, or overnight. Again, open any covered holes with a tapestry needle.

Working the Shin in Flamestitch: Cut an 8″ length of Serica. Separate the plies of silk and straighten each one. Lay 3 plies next to each other and thread them on a #24 needle. For added luster, keep strands flat, or side by side, while you stitch. Refer to the Chart for Stitching and Beading. Starting from the bottom right corner of the marked canvas (where the Bottom Flap, Back Flap, and Front sections meet), count up 1 horizontal canvas thread and over 9 vertical canvas threads to the left. Begin stitching the letter "Shin" at this point. Work one color at a time, referring to the chart and the key for color, direction and length of each stitch (the number of

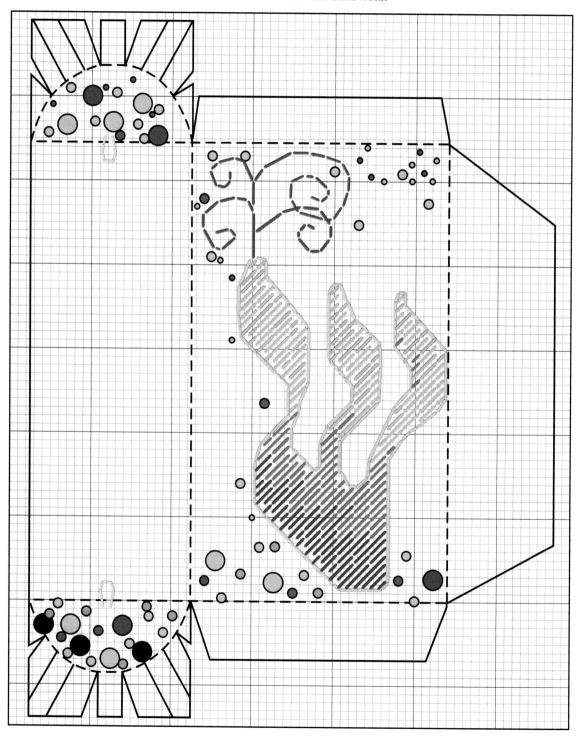

LACING DIAGRAM FOR THE TOP

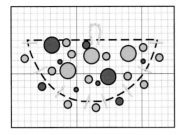

LACING DIAGRAM FOR THE BOTTOM

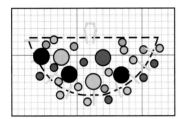

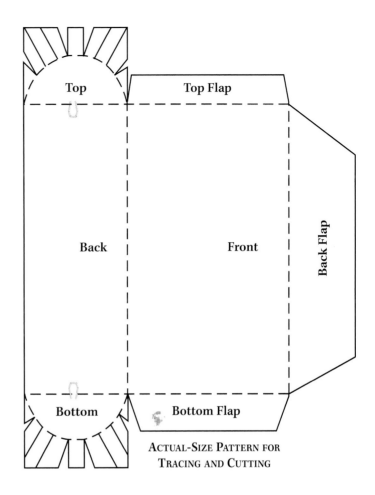

ACTUAL-SIZE PATTERN FOR
TRACING AND CUTTING

KEY

Flamestitch, Wrapped Backstitch
with Kreinik Silk Serica
━ Medium Dark Cerulean #5105
━ Medium Teal #4044
━ Light Teal #4043
━ Light Cobalt Violet #1043
━ Dark Cobalt Violet #1046

Couching, Hanging Loops, Beading, Lacing
with Kreinik Metallic Threads
━ Medium Braid #16 in Gold #002
━ Cable #002P in Gold

Beadwork with Mill Hill Beads
Pebble Beads
⬤ New Penny #05555
⬤ Old Gold #00557
⬤ Amethyst #05202
⬤ Midnight Rainbow #05086
Glass Seed Beads
⬤ Abalone Antique #03037
⬤ Gold #00557
⬤ Old Rose #00553
Petite Glass Seed Beads
⬤ Gold #40557
⬤ Old Rose #40553

continued

intersections of canvas threads it crosses). To start, hold the tail end of the silk down in back with one hand and work stitches over it to secure; do not make knots.

Note: Silk is very strong. Keep it taut as you work. Some stitchers dampen the silk threads by running them over a moist paper towel to "relax" them. If the plies should get tangled as you work, remove the needle, separate and smooth the plies, and then rethread the needle.

Working the Spirals in Wrapped Backstitch: Using Serica in Dark Cobalt Violet and a #24 needle, start a backstitch in the same hole as the last flamestitch, at the top left of the Shin. (Anchor the silk on the back by running the needle under a few flamestitches.) Work one spiral, following the chart. At the end of the spiral, with the needle on the front, wrap the last backstitch by placing the needle under it from right to left. Be careful not to split the silk with your needle as you tunnel under the stitch. Tunnel under the second-to-last stitch, again from right to left. If backstitches cover more than one thread, make more than one wrap along them. Continue wrapping stitches in the first spiral. When you have returned to the beginning, bring the silk to the wrong side and weave it under a few flamestitches. Work each of the 4 spirals individually.

Outlining the Shin with Couching: Do not cut the gold Braid, but simply thread the end of the reel with a #24 needle. Insert the threaded needle from the front above the final row of stitches (upper left side of the Shin). Remove the needle and hold about $\frac{1}{2}''$ of Braid against the back of the canvas. Cut an 8″ length of Cable. Separate the plies slowly so they won't tangle. (Each wrapped ply consists of a fiber strand and a metallic strand. Do not unwrap these strands.) Thread 1 ply through a #26 needle. Use this strand to couch the Braid, referring to the stitch detail on page 124. Unwrap the Braid from the reel as you couch with the Cable. Make the Braid follow the outline of the Shin in graceful curves as you fasten it in place. When you get almost all the way around the Shin, cut the Braid a few inches longer than necessary. Use a #24 needle to bring the Braid end to the back. Weave the braid under the silk to secure it, and complete the couching.

Beading: Use 1 ply of Cable and a #26 needle. Refer to the chart and key for type and approximate position of beads. Secure the pebble beads first, then the seed beads, followed by the petite seed beads. To anchor the Cable, start with a cross stitch from the back, place a bead in position and bring the Cable through the bead 2 times. If you have enough Cable left on the needle, carry it across the back to secure the next bead. When attaching the seed beads and petite beads, use a #28 needle.

Attaching Hanging Loops: Use 8″ of Braid with a #24 needle to make a hanging loop for the top and another for the bottom of the case. Make a knot at the end of the Braid and attach where indicated on the pattern or chart. To keep the loop open, place the pointed end of a pencil halfway through it. Bring the Braid through to the wrong side and make a second knot.

Assembly: Cut carefully on the solid lines with sharp scissors. Fold the canvas along the dash lines, one section at a time, beginning at the top. Start by folding the Top Flap to the wrong side, and crease the edge. Next, fold back the straight edge of the semi-circular Top on a 90º angle. Fold each tab 90 º back from the Top, and mold the Front around the semi-circular edge of the Top to check the fit. The Front should meet smoothly with the Top all the way around to the Back Flap. Play with this curve until it is smooth, but be aware that the lacing will pull everything together. Remove excess canvas from the tabs to reduce bulk. Use 1 strand of Cable and a beading needle to lace, or whipstitch the Front to the Top. Follow the Lacing Diagram for the Top, stitching beads to the edge in between whip-stitches. Work loose stitches to allow room to maneuver the needle from hole to hole, then later, tighten the earlier stitches. Fasten off the Cable. Work the Bottom in the same way, following the Lacing Diagram for the Bottom.

Finishing: Fold the Back Flap over the Back. Make ties to close the case: Use a #24 needle to sew 8″ strands of buttonhole floss to the Back Flap at 2 evenly spaced locations. Stitch ties to the Back to correspond. Insert the prayer scroll, then tie the floss strands together and clip them short. ✧

STAR OF DAVID
BOOKMARKS

Dimensions: Stars, 1¼" and 1½"; braided tail, 8" or as desired

Materials & Tools

- Boye size #11 steel crochet hook
  For Silvery Bookmark shown at upper right:
- DMC Metallic Thread, 1 spool each Silver #285 (A) and Rainbow #275 (B)
  For Variegated Bookmark shown at lower left:
- DMC Tatting Thread, 1 spool each Variegated Blue, color #103 (C) and Variegated Purple, color #52 (D)
- DMC Metallic Thread, 1 spool each Silver #285 (E) and Light Gold #282 (F)

Directions

Note: For Crochet Abbreviations, see page 72.

SILVERY BOOKMARK

First Triangle: With A, ch 33, keeping ch flat, sl st to form a ring.

Round 1: Ch 3, 4 dc in slip st, 1 dc in next 10 ch, 5 dc in next ch, 1 dc in each of next 10 ch, 5 dc in next ch, 1 dc in each of next 10 ch (keeping triangle flat), sl st to top of ch 3; end off.

Round 2: With B, sl st in first (joining) dc of previous rd, skip 1 dc, work *5 dc shell in next dc, skip dc, sc in next dc, skip 1 dc, 3 dc in next dc, skip 1 dc, sc in next dc, skip 1 dc, 3 dc in next dc, skip 1 dc, sc in next dc, skip 1 dc, 3 dc in next dc, skip 1 dc, sc in next dc (three 3 dc shells) skip 1 dc*. Repeat from * to *, ending with sl st into beginning of round. Pull ends tightly and weave them in and out of a few stitches, then clip excess thread. This completes the first triangle.

Second Triangle: With B, ch 33. Weave into the first triangle as in figure 1, then sl st to form a ring. Pulling the chain around as you work with B, repeat round 1 above. When you make the last dc, flatten out the crochet work just completed, as shown in figure 2.

When work is flat, and all stitches are face up and intertwined but not twisted, sl st to top of ch 3. End off.

With A, repeat round 2, ending with sl st into beginning st of round. Weave thread ends in and out of a few stitches, then clip excess thread.

Pull on points to flatten and adjust points to form the star.

Braid: Cut 48" long strands: 4 A, 5 B. Hold them together. Insert crochet hook into the outside round of the star, at an inside angle between two points. Grab the center of the cut strands, and pull up a loop. Insert ends of strands into loop to make a lark's head knot. You now have eighteen 24" long strands Divide strands into 3 groups of 6 strands, and braid tightly and flatly. It is helpful to have a partner hold the star, so you can keep the strands taut for braiding. Knot the end of the braid, and cut the thread ends even, ½" beyond the knot.

Figure 1

Figure 2

STAR OF DAVID BOOKMARKS
continued

VARIEGATED BOOKMARK

First and Second Triangles: Follow the directions above, substituting one strand C and E held together for A, and one strand D and F held together for B.
Braid: 15 strands: Cut 48" long strands: 2 each of C and D, 4 strands each of E and F.

Following the directions for braiding on page 79, attach with a lark's head knot. Divide into 3 groups of 8 strands. Finish in the same manner. ♦

HANNUKAH MENORAH

Dimensions: 4¹/₄" wide by 1³/₄" high by 1³/₄" deep

Materials & Tools
- *3 packages of Peach Granitex, by Polyform*
- *Gold Rub 'n Buff*
- *Wood skewers, toothpicks*
- *Small piece of balsa wood*
- *Craft knife*
- *Needles or pins*
- *1" bristle brush*
- *Birthday candles*

Directions

Preparation: Begin by whittling a few tools from wooden skewers and balsa in order to press holes for windows, doorways, etc. into the clay. For example, use a craft knife to square off the blunt end of one wood skewer to make a shape for a rectangular or arched window hole. Carve the other tools according to your taste and needs.

Read "Working with Polymer Clay" on page 18. Granitex has a stone-like look but is similar to Sculpey in malleability.

Sculpting: Soften the Granitex and roll out a sheet approximately ¹/₂" thick. Cut a 2¹/₂" x 2" piece for a center back wall, and curve the sides toward the front slightly. Also, cut out 4 rectangles ¹/₂" wide and of varying heights shorter than the center back wall, and place 2 at either end of it. Refer to the actual-size diagram opposite, which shows the construction from above. For candle holders/terra cotta pots, roll eight ¹/₂" balls and press them onto the top of the back piece and side rectangles. Press the end of a birthday candle into each ball to make holes that fit the candles. Wrap a narrow snake around the candle, for a rim on each pot.

For the city, create several rectangular layers of clay. Press smaller rectangles onto the layers for buildings and alleyways. Top one with a half-ball, for a dome. Use sticks and tools to press in doorways, windows, steps, and jagged rocks. Add smaller details with toothpicks and pins. Make sure each piece is firmly joined to the one below. Place one ³/₄" block near the front of the city to hold the Shamash, or helper candle. Make a candle holder/terra cotta pot in the same manner as before and place it on this low block.

Finishing: When satisfied with your design, bake and cool it according to the manufacturer's instructions. Dip a stiff brush into the Rub 'n Buff, wipe off most of the paste onto a rag or paper towel, and with this mostly dry brush, lightly gild the menorah. Build up a more brilliant gold by brushing some areas more than once. ♦

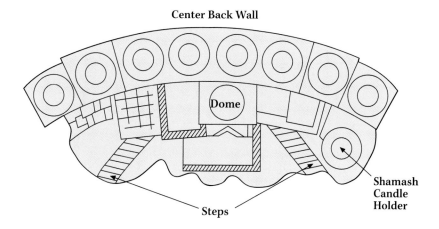

Center Back Wall

Dome

Shamash Candle Holder

Steps

BOTTLE BREASTPLATES

Dimensions: Wine and Le Vin (French for "the Wine") tags, 1¼″ x ⅞″; Pesach (Hebrew for Passover) and L'Chaim (Hebrew for "to Life") tags, 1 ¾″ x 1¼″, Fruit of the Vine, 2″ x ⅝″

Materials & Tools

- Aleene's Opake Shrink-It shrink art plastic sheet
- Crystal Waterproof Ink Pad, in black*
- Le Plume II by Marvy Uchida water based markers in Victorian colors 1122-12C*
- Fine-tip permanent ink markers in black, red, green, blue
- foot chain (ball or link)
- Jump rings or fine wire
- Cynthia Hart Sentimental Frame #596-F* and Rose Frame #619*
- Cynthia Hart Victorian Banner #A1650F*
- Fiskars Paper Edgers: Victorian and Scallop
- Wire cutters, jewelry or needle nose pliers
- Fine sandpaper
- Hole punch
- Oven (a toaster oven may be used)
- Cookie sheet (or, for a toaster oven, a piece of posterboard or matboard)
- Spatula, oven mitt
- Round jar
- Optional: Beadworks clear frosted glass lampwork teardrop beads on wire loops D24

*From Rubber Stampede

BOTTLE BREASTPLATES

continued

Directions

Preparation: Lightly sand one side of shrink art plastic sheet, (hereafter indicated as plastic) for better adhesion of pigments.

Stamping: Press the stamp onto the ink pad, moving the stamp around to ensure that the entire design becomes inked. Press the stamp firmly onto the plastic, leaving a $1\frac{1}{2}''$ margin all around. When removing the stamp, lift it straight up to avoid smudging. Let ink set for a few minutes.

Lettering: Choose a message for your label(s); you may use one of the patterns shown here, or you may write your own personalized label. To design your own, stamp the inked frame design on scrap paper, and use a pencil and ruler to draw guidelines inside the frame. Pencil in straight, even letters, adjusting the spacing or size of the letters as needed. When you are satisfied with the lettering, go over them with black marker. Place plastic over the lettering pattern, centering it within the frame of the stamped design. Trace the letters onto the plastic using a fine, permanent ink marker.

Coloring: Use markers to color design elements or shade backgrounds. Refer to the back of the stamp for a suggested treatment. Color flowers, leaves, borders. Be aware that colors will intensify as the piece bakes and shrinks and therefore backgrounds should be kept light.

Cutting: Cut out the design as follows: For an interesting shape such as the Victorian Banner, follow the outlines but do not make intricate cuts into the corners, where tassels and notches are very tightly spaced. Use scissors that provide decorative edges for the rectangular frames, cutting slightly outside the design for the Sentimental Frame, and $\frac{1}{2}''$ beyond the design for the Rose Frame. Punch holes into the upper corners of each piece.

Finishing: Place pieces, well spaced, on a cookie sheet. If you are using a toaster oven, cut a piece of posterboard or matboard that will fit inside to use as a baking sheet. Bake pieces in an oven preheated to 275° Fahrenheit. Pieces will curl as they shrink, and then flatten out after about 3 minutes. When they are flat, the piece is done. Remove the cookie sheet from the oven and quickly lift off the plastic using a spatula. If you wish your piece to be gently curved, for example, to follow the contours of a wine bottle, then immediately place the hot plastic face down on your oven mitt-covered hand, and press the curved surface of a bottle or jar onto it. Let the piece cool for a few minutes.

Use pliers to open jump rings. Insert one into a punched hole on the tag, and then into a link of chain. Alternatively, cut small pieces of wire to run through the punched hole and wrap into a link of chain. Use pliers to close up rings, or twist and curl wire ends for safe handling. If desired, attach ball chain end caps or use jump rings to add beads with loops. ◇

Actual-Size Patterns for Bottle Breastplate Lettering

BOTTLE STOPPERS

Dimensions: 2½" to 3" high

Materials & Tools

- Fimo Modeling Material* (hereafter referred to as "clay"): Pink, Light Turquoise, Red
- Silver and gold powder*
- Beadworks beads: as shown at top, starting at left, 5 Japanese lampwork beads with silver foil inserts G11, 5 heavy metal beads AN06; at center, Venetian-style and foiled glass lamp bead B41; at right, Venetian-style and foiled glass lamp beads K37 and H41-9mm
- Ball chain
- Gold ball beads, 5mm
- Headpins
- Bottle corks (available from hardware stores) to fit bottle
- Wood screw, 1½" in length
- Wood glue
- Baking sheet
- Oven
- Screwdriver

  * From AMACO

Directions

Sculpting: Read "Working with Polymer Clay" on page 18. These designs atop corks are free-form pieces, so refer to the photograph for ideas, but also experiment with clay colors, color combinations, beads and shapes.

Begin with a walnut-sized piece of clay formed into a ball. Sink a screw into it so that the head is buried, then smooth over the opening. As shown in the center design, you may wish to insert the screw shank through the center of a clay disk as well. Flatten the bottom of the clay design so that it will make full contact with the top surface of the cork.

Adding Beads: Keep the sides of the main ball of the design free of beads that protrude: This area will be squeezed when pulling or twisting the stopper, causing any beads not firmly and well-attached there to fall off. To attach beads to the top, use brads, or trim headpins with clippers so they may be inserted through one or two beads and into the clay. Attach several beads in this way to form a clustered crown. Consider making contrast-color beads from clay and attaching them in the same manner. Beads may be also be secured by pressing them halfway into the clay, like the heavy metal beads. The ball chain was simply wrapped around the clay, trimmed with clippers to the desired length, and pressed so it sinks into the clay.

Finishing: If desired, dip a finger into metallic powder and apply over some surfaces of clay. Bake and cool the design on the screw according to the manufacturer's instructions. Push a nail into the cork as a pilot hole for the screw; remove the nail. Apply glue to the wide end of the cork. Gently twist the screw into the pilot hole. Let the glue dry completely. ◊

Chapter Four

Vignettes

In the Victorian era, dollhouses were built for the wealthy, either as playthings for the children, or as a means of displaying collections of miniature objects of value. Just last year, Christie's auctioned off seventeen miniature rooms, each by a different designer; prices were in the five-figures. While none of us may afford—or care—to live in such splendid chambers, we take great delight in idealizing wondrous environments in small scale.

Many of the designs that follow, in a scale where one inch represents one foot, would be a master stroke inside a dollhouse. However, let's not discount the pleasure of happening upon a Lilliputian scene in an unexpected location—an occasional table in an entryway, along a shelf, or as a place setting at a special dinner.

Fit for a Queen

While this mini quilt by Judi Kauffman is just the right size for a typical dollhouse double bed, it is such a pièce-de-resistance that I could not resist setting it within a 9 x 12-inch frame. Judi began with foundation piecing, crazy quilt style, then added a small abundance of embroidery using Bucilla's silk ribbons, the occasional bauble and beadwork.

Bedside Manners

Mini brass stencils from American Traditional Stencils are the secret behind this trio of dreamy dollhouse pieces. A rose bouquet and a garland motif used on fabric give the look of elegant appliqué to a doll quilt. A few rows of tiny hand stitches add dimension and classic elegance. The same bouquet stencil applied to a non-woven fabric simulates needlepoint in an oval rug. For a finishing touch, add fringe to the rug with a cut and unraveled length of grosgrain ribbon. The flower basket picture is embroidered, but it is stenciling that marks the pattern underneath, to aid in positioning every lazy daisy or outline stitch. Barbara E. Swanson, who designed these projects, was very resourceful in providing a frame for her little masterpiece: unable to find one just the right size, she cut strips from modeling compound, then pressed a design into the strips using another mini brass stencil.

Vignettes

Petite Grannies

Experts in the field of miniatures often remark that Linda Driscoll does the finest and smallest crochet work. Her hooks are filed down by a jeweler so that she can produce her most intricate pieces. For this book, she thinks many 88 *readers will rise to the challenge of using a number 11 crochet hook and DMC Machine Embroidery Thread to make the little afghan with the ivory background, at left. However, if your fingers are less than nimble and even your corrected eyesight less than perfect, Linda*

suggests following the same pattern—but with a number 14 hook and DMC tatting thread. The afghan at right, this time with a black background, shows the result. This piece may be laid across a double doll bed, with a generous overhang at the sides. Look closely, and you will notice a variation in the edgings: a demure scallop for the tiny afghan, a lacy shell with picot points for the small one. For each matching pillow, simply make an extra granny motif, edging and sewing it to two joined and stuffed satin squares.

89

Vanity Fair

The matchbox drawers of the dressing table really open—designer Kathryn Severns keeps her rings, pierced earring studs and backs inside. The pull-up stool conceals a jar of night cream under its skirt. It sits upon a rectangular rug, painted by Barbara E. Swanson for American Traditional Stencils. To little glass jars

that once held bouillon cubes or artichoke hearts, I applied either rose motifs from the same sheet of Victorian stickers used for the dressing table and stool, or a ring of dried rosebuds. Tied with sheer ribbon at the rim, these jars make sweet containers for potpourri, little soaps, cotton balls, bath salts, or votive candles.

91

Vignettes

Come Into My Parlor

A Victorian salon by the end of the nineteenth century exhibited the taste for exotic, far-eastern interior design. Kathleen George swathed Sculpey III modeling compound on balsa wood frames for the slipper chair, sofa, and armchair. She draped contrasting colors, added beads, passementerie trim. Rubber stamps were impressed to feign the texture of cut velvet or lush upholstery; for the sides of the hexagonal table, a stamp was used to simulate mosaic. The butler's table is a graceful, three-legged pedestal. A bit of the same "clay" anchors an artificial plant in each of the smaller pots. By the way, the tassel looped onto the key on the table is but a variation of the holiday ornament shown on pages 57 and 59.

SIXTEEN FAMOUS EUROPEAN PLAYS
CERF & CARTMELL
JIM FOBEL'S DIET FEASTS
DRAMA

By the Chimney
with Care

*Kathleen George was the architect
and mason for this chimney. Built of
Styrofoam and covered with
plaster and stones, it incorporates a
standard bookend bracket. Its rustic
charm supports its year-round
service, but at Christmas time, you
may wish to add some evergreens,
and hang a couple of tiny stockings.
These, by Penny Kimball using DMC
rayon and metallic threads, feature
a cross-stitch Tin Soldier and
Nutcracker. Each will just hold a
rolled up bill, or a piece of penny
candy. Hush—don't let the elves know,
but oh, what marvelous gifts await
them. Notice the knitted stockings on
the chair and the gift wrapping in
process. Turn the page for a
better look.*

Help Your Elf

The story of the Shoemaker and the Elves prompted Michele Maks Thompson to design tiny apparel brimming with folkloric charm. Michele writes, "As a child I was fascinated by the possibility of meeting one of these wee people; as an adult I have the skill to actually construct the clothing for them. I imagined the shoemaker's wife making traditional peasant's garments, but adding a bit of glittery

trim to show her appreciation for all their help." Stockinette stitch and garter stitch using J. & P. Coats Knit-Cro-Sheen and Coats & Clark Southmaid keep these pieces simple to knit, even with number 1 needles.

Picture them dressing a five-inch doll, clipped along a clothesline string for a unique Christmas garland, or even individually hung from little hooks for an array of holiday ornaments.

Fairy Houses

Summer and winter centerpieces are guaranteed to stir the imagination and the conversation at the dining table. Inspired by the motion picture "Fairy Tale," designer Michele Maks Thompson set about cutting bases from slabs and shapes of Styrofoam. Next, she spread them with a mossy ground

Vignettes

cover of sawdust and paint or a blanket of spackling compound and crystal "snow." Natural materials from the garden, dried florals from the crafts store, plus an odd charm, bead, and handful of gravel, endow them with primitive, whimsical charm. No one would be surprised to find a tiny sprite at home in either of these enchanting shelters!

ELEGANT MINI QUILT

Dimensions:

6$\frac{5}{8}$" by 8$\frac{1}{4}$", not including a $\frac{3}{4}$" lace ruffle

Materials & Tools

- 8$\frac{1}{2}$" x 11" sheet Fun-dation transparent quilt block piecing material from Handler Textile Corp.
- Fat quarter of fine woven fabric for backing and binding, shown here: celadon polished cotton
- Assorted scraps of fine woven fabrics or wide ribbons, in colors as shown or as desired: brocades, moires and mock moires, lace and mock laces, white-on-white designs
- Bucilla 100% Silk Ribbon, 1 package each: Ivory #1321, 13mm; Variegated Antique Copper #1303, 13mm; Light Mauve #550, 7mm; Forest Green #545, 7mm; Forest Green #628, 4mm; Lichen #618, 4mm; Coral #537, 4mm
- From Mill Hill: Petite Seed Beads: 1 package each Heather Mauve #42024 and Cream #40123; Glass Treasures: 5-Petal Flowers in Matte Amethyst #12007, Matte Rose #12008, and Very Petite Flowers in Amethyst #12150; Medium Leaves in Matte Olive #12144; Ivory Cameo Heart #12066
- Kreinik Medium Braid #16 in Star Pink #092

- Ivory pearls, 3mm, from Sulyn Industries
- Ivory lace bow applique, 1" x 1$\frac{3}{8}$", from St. Louis Trimmings
- $\frac{1}{2}$ yard ivory lace trim 1" wide, for ruffle
- Ivory and rose sewing thread
- Bucilla chenille needles
- Beading and sewing needles, straight pins
- Sewing machine
- Fabric marking pen (Sakura Micron Pigma fine line marker was used for this project)
- Iron

Directions

Foundation Piecing: Place transparent foundation piecing material over the actual-size pattern for foundation piecing, and trace all lines and numbers. Add a $\frac{5}{16}$" border all around, for the binding. Since you will be working from the wrong side, the finished quilt design will be a mirror image of what appears on these drawn lines. Turn the foundation to the wrong side.

Cut a piece of fabric at least $\frac{1}{4}$" larger all around than Section 1 of the design. Pin this fabric right side up over Section 1. From another fabric, cut out a piece at least $\frac{1}{4}$" larger all around than Section 2 of the design. Place the fabric for Section 2 on top of Section 1, with the right sides of the fabrics together, and with both fabrics overlapping the line between Section 1 and Section 2. To check placements before stitching, place a pin along the line common to both sections, and fold the second fabric over to its right side. Make sure it covers Section 2 and has seam allowances all around.

Turn the piece over so that you can see the marked lines of the foundation, and move the pin. Place the layers underneath the presser foot of the sewing machine. Start stitching just before the marked line, continue to stitch along the line, and stop 1 or 2 stitches beyond the line. For stitches at the edge of quilt top, stitch into the binding area. Carefully trim the seam allowances to $\frac{1}{4}$". Fold the second fabric over to the right side to cover Section 2 on the foundation, and press the seam.

Position a third fabric over Section 3, then flip it over onto the first and second fabrics, and stitch along the line between joined Sections 1 and 2, and Section 3, in the same manner as before. Trim the seam allowance, fold back the third fabric, and press the seam. Continue in this manner, adding different

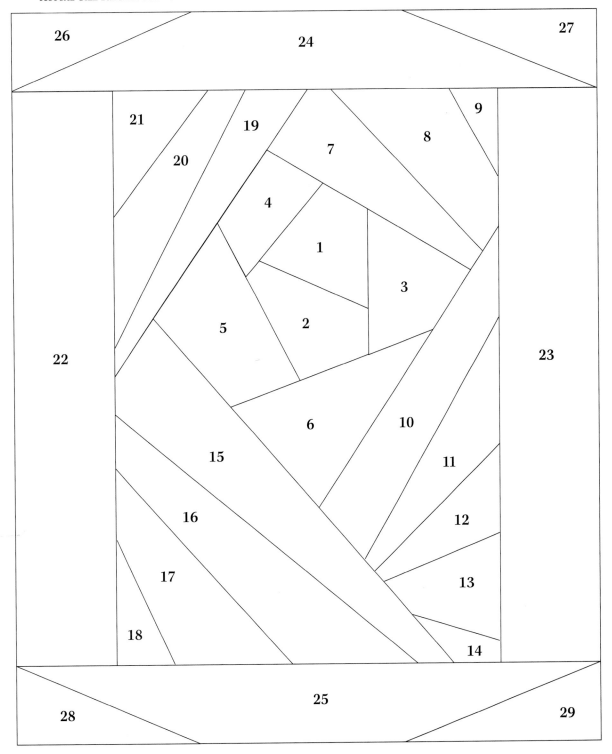

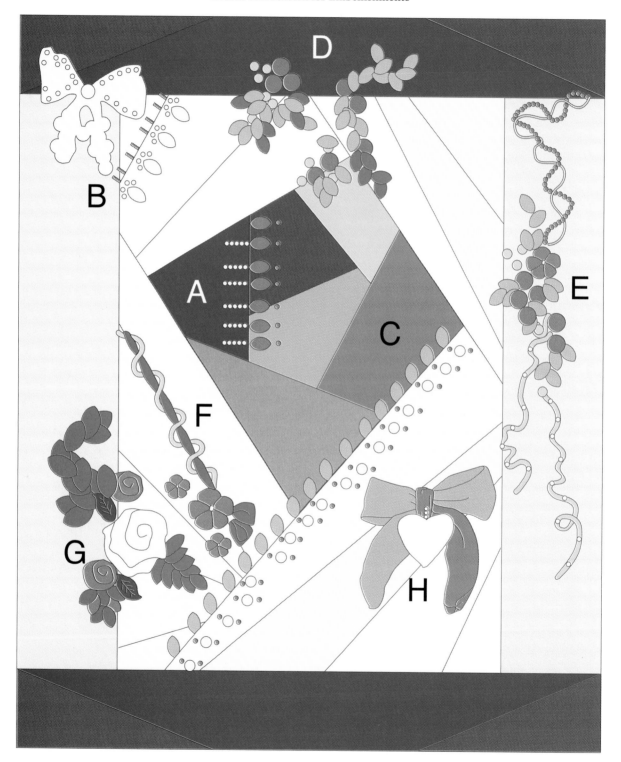

KEY

Area A

- Straight Stitch with Light Mauve ribbon
- ○ Cream Petite Seed Beads on a long straight st.
- ◉ Mauve Petite Seed Bead

Area B

- Straight stitch with Ivory ribbon
- ▭ Straight stitch with Medium Braid
- ○ Cream Petite Seed Beads
- Applique, Cream Petite Seed Beads, 3mm Pearl

Area C

- Japanese ribbon stitch with Lichen ribbon
- ○ 3mm Pearl
- ◉ Heather Mauve Petite Seed Bead

Area D

- French knot with Light Mauve ribbon
- French knot with Coral ribbon
- Jap. ribbon st. with 4mm Forest Green ribbon
- Jap. ribbon stitch with Lichen ribbon

Area E: Same as Area D, plus

- Coral ribbon with Cream Petite Seed Beads
- ▬ Medium Braid couched with pink thread
- ⬤⬤⬤⬤⬤ String of Heather Mauve Petite Seed Beads, couched with pink thread
- Amethyst Glass Flower with Cream Petite Seed Bead

Area F

- Running stitches ending in two 3/8" loops, with 7mm Forest Green ribbon
- Coral ribbon woven through the running sts.
- Matte Rose Glass Flower, Cream Pet. Seed Bd.
- Very Petite Amethyst Glass Flower, Cream Petite Seed Bead

Area G

- Folded Rose using Ivory ribbon
- Gathered rosette using Light Mauve ribbon
- Glass Leaf
- Straight stitch with Light Mauve ribbon
- Jap. ribbon st. with 4mm Forest Green ribbon

Area H

- Bow of Variegated Antique Copper ribbon
- Cameo Heart with Cream Petite Seed Beads

fabrics to adjacent sections, and working in numerical order. For depth, use darker colors for sections 1-6, light colors for sections 7-21, frame the design with fabrics that incorporate light and dark colors for sections 22 and 23, then use the same darker colors again for sections 24-29. Refer to the photograph for a suggested arrangement of colors.

Embellishment: Work one lettered area at a time. Use the seam lines on the actual-size pattern for embellishment to help pinpoint the location for each ribbon embroidery stitch. Within each area, work the ribbon embroidery first, using a chenille needle. Refer to the key, the photograph, and the stitch details on pages 124-125. End cascades, streamers, or long lengths of ribbon with the Japanese ribbon stitch. Next, embroider with the braid. After the embroidery is completed in an area, sew on any appliques, using matching thread. Add beads, pearls, and glass flowers and leaves, positioning them in relation to the ribbons; use a beading needle and doubled sewing thread to match the embellishment or the background.

To make a gathered rosette, use a sewing needle, 3" of silk ribbon, and thread to match the ribbon. Make tiny running stitches following the diagram below, then pull the thread to gather the ribbon

tightly. The ribbon will begin to spiral on its own, but take a few stitches to tack the rounds of gathers at the base of the flower. Make sure the ribbon ends are tucked neatly underneath as well. Keep the needle in place and use the remaining thread to stitch the flower to the quilt top.

Assembly: Cut out the foundation and patchwork fabric along the outer marked lines. Measure and cut fabric for the backing (which will form a self-binding), 5/8" larger than the quilt top all around. Fold the raw edges 1/4" to the wrong side, and press to crease. Center the quilt top on the backing fabric, with wrong sides together. Fold up the sides of the backing 3/8" over the quilt top, covering the edges. Pin to secure. Fold up the top and bottom edges of the backing in the same way; pin. Use tiny slip stitches to sew the folded backing edges to the quilt top, for a self-binding. Gather lace trimming to fit across the top of the quilt, and slip-stitch it securely in place. ◊

Stenciled Quilt

Dimensions: 7″ x 7″

Materials & Tools

- American Traditional Stencils: Trousseau (MS-11), Triple Border (FS-930), and Bow & Heart (MS-214)
- 8″ square of finely woven ecru fabric; used here: Zweigart Jubilee #ZP232, 28-count even-weave fabric in Ivory #225
- 7″ square of low loft batting
- 8″ square of lightweight, bleached muslin
- DecoArt Easy Blend Stencil Paints: Cadmium Yellow (DEB03), Raspberry Pink (DEB11), Wedgewood Blue (DEB19), and Holly Green (DEB32)
- Ecru sewing thread
- Anchor Marlitt Rayon Floss in Off White #1212
- Ruler
- Low-tack masking tape
- 4 stencil brushes, $^3/_{16}$″ in diameter
- Paper towels
- Sewing needle and pins
- Sewing machine (optional)
- Disappearing marker pen

Directions

Preparation: Using a disappearing marker and ruler, mark a 7″ square on fabric for quilt top, with $^1/_2$″ margins all around. Also mark the center, mark a line $^1/_2$″ from the marked outline on one short side (for the head of the bed), and lines 1″ from the marked outline along the other three sides, for a border line.

Stenciling: Read the "Stenciling Know-How," on the oposite page. Refer to the photograph for positioning and to the Oval Rug directions on page 105 for suggested colors. Position the Trousseau stencil to the left of the center mark. Tape it to secure, and stencil with the paints. Stencil a second motif to the right of center. Stencil leaves to fill in the empty spaces at the top and bottom of this stenciled area. Center the bow of the Bow & Heart stencil on the line marked at the head of the quilt top. Stencil with pink and blue. Stencil a single rose with leaves centered under the bow. Place the vine from the Triple Border stencil along one of the border lines. Stencil randomly with yellow and then blue. Complete the vine motif with green. Repeat this process to create a vine along all the border lines. Use pink and green to stencil single sprigs of mini-flowers from the Trousseau stencil along the inside curves of the vine. Allow paint to dry for 24 hours, then heat-set the paint according to the manufacturer's instructions.

Assembly: Center the muslin backing right side up over the batting. Place the stenciled quilt top, right side down, on top. Pin the layers to secure. Stitch the layers together along the marked outlines for the 7″ square (if visible), or $^1/_2$″ from the edges, leaving 2″ unstitched along the head edge. Trim seam allowances to $^1/_4$″; clip the corners. Turn quilt right side out with the batting in the middle. Turn open edges $^1/_4$″ to the inside and slip-stitch closed. Lightly press.

Quilting: Use a ruler and disappearing marker to mark quilting lines on the quilt top as follows: Beginning at the center, mark a vertical line from the head of the quilt to the bottom edge; interrupt line for stenciled areas. Mark parallel lines at $^1/_2$″ intervals, but do not mark beyond the side borders. In each bottom lower corner, mark three angled lines creating a "fan." Mark horizontal lines $^1/_2$″ apart along the sides, beyond the stenciled border. Quilt along these lines with one strand of floss, making running stitches as tiny and even as you can. ◊

OVAL RUG

Dimensions: 2 ½" x 4, not including ¼" fringe all around

Materials & Tools

- *American Traditional Stencils: Trousseau (MS-11)*
- *Small piece of Kreative Kanvas, from Kunin Felt*
- *Americana acrylic paint* in Buttermilk (DA3)*
- *Heavenly Hues acrylic paint* in Country Blue (DHH11)*
- *Easy Blend Stencil Paints* in Cadmium Yellow (DEB03), Raspberry Pink (DEB11), Wedgewood Blue (DEB19), and Holly Green (DEB32)*
- *Matte Varnish**
- *⅜ yard ecru grosgrain ribbon, ⅞" wide*
- *Thick tacky glue*
- *Pencil, ruler, tracing paper*
- *Paintbrushes, 1" flat and ¼" flat*
- *Several cotton swabs*
- *Low-tack masking tape*
- *4 stencil brushes, ³/₁₆" in diameter*
- *Paper towels*

  *From DecoArt

Actual-Size Half Pattern for Oval Rug

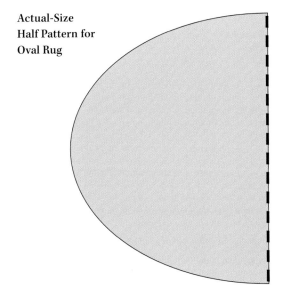

Directions

Preparation: Trace the actual-size oval half pattern onto folded tracing paper, with dash lines along the fold. Fold the tracing paper along the dash lines, then cut out and unfold the complete pattern. Trace the oval outline onto canvas with a pencil; cut out the canvas. Paint one side of the canvas with two coats of Buttermilk paint, allowing it to dry after each coat. Working freehand, paint a ⁵/₁₆"-wide border around the edges, using a ¼" brush and Country Blue paint. Wipe off the excess with a cotton swab. Allow to dry.

Stenciling: Read the "Stenciling Know-How," on page 50. Refer to the photograph for suggested colors and positioning. Position the stencil to the left of center. Tape to secure and stencil with the Easy Blend Paints. Use yellow for the rose centers and some of the leaves. Add pink to flowers and some leaf tips. Use blue to create shadows on some of the leaves and flower petals. Complete the design with green over all of the leaves. Repeat to create a second motif on the right side. Stencil a single rose motif (with leaves) two times, to fill the center space. Allow to dry for 24 hours.

Finishing: Apply 2 to 3 coats of varnish, allowing to dry between coats. For fringe, cut away ⅛" from one selvage edge of ribbon. Use a pin to pull out threads that run along the length of the ribbon, stopping ¼" from the remaining selvage edge. Glue this selvage edge to the back of the canvas, so that the fringe extends beyond the edges. Let dry, then trim the fringe to ⅜" all around. ❧

FLOWER BASKET PICTURE

Dimensions: 2¼" x 3¼"

Materials & Tools

- Fimo* modeling material in Gold (hereafter referred to as "clay")
- Rub 'n Buff* in Antique White
- 4" square of finely woven ecru fabric; used here: Zweigart Jubilee #ZP232, 28 count even-weave fabric in Ivory #225
- 4" square of low loft batting
- DecoArt Easy Blend Stencil Paints in Cadmium Yellow (DEB03), Raspberry Pink (DEB11), Wedgewood Blue (DEB19), and Holly Green (DEB32)
- Anchor Marlitt Rayon Floss in Gold #1078, Light Blue #1059, Light Rose #1019, Rose #1207, Medium Green #897, and Lavender #816
- Goop glue*
- Rolling pin
- Craft knife
- Ruler
- American Traditional Stencils: Flower Basket (MS-64) and Grapes & Scroll (MS-210)
- Low-tack masking tape
- 4 stencil brushes ³⁄₁₆" in diameter
- Paper towels
- Tapestry needle

*From AMACO

Directions

Stenciling: Center the Flower Basket stencil over the fabric square. Referring to the "Stenciling Know-How," on page 50, stencil the design. Because the stenciling may not be completely covered by subsequent embroidery stitches, use similar colors for paint and floss. Refer to the photograph for suggested colors. Allow paint to dry for 24 hours. Heat-set the paint, according to the manufacturer's instructions.

Embroidery: Refer to the stitch details on page 124. With one strand of gold floss, backstitch the stems and basket rims, and straight-stitch along the lattice weave of the basket. Using 2 strands of light blue floss, make a lazy daisy stitch for each petal of the 4 outer flowers. Stitch a French knot at the center of each of these flowers, using 2 strands of lavender. For the 3 remaining flowers, satin-stitch the center petals with one strand of light rose, and then use one strand of rose to surround the center with lazy daisy stitches and French knots. Use one strand of medium green floss to make tiny backstitches at each intersection of lattices on the basket, and straight stitches for the leaves.

Making a Frame: Read "Working with Polymer Clay," on page 18. Soften clay and roll it to an ¹⁄₈" thickness. Use a ruler and craft knife to cut a 2¼" x 3¼" rectangle, for the picture back, and four ³⁄₈" wide strips: two 3" long and two 4" long, for the frame front. Center the scroll stencil over one strip. Press it into the clay. Remove the stencil and repeat for the remaining strips. Miter the ends. Set aside. Roll remaining clay into an ¹⁄₈" snake. Lay the snakes along the edges of the frame back, joining the ends at a corner and trimming away any excess. Press the snake lightly to adhere it in place. Use the back of the craft knife to incise diagonal lines into the snake, to give it the texture of rope. Bake the five frame sections according to the manufacturer's instructions. Let cool, then accent the strips and rope with Rub 'n Buff.

Assembly: Trim the embroidered fabric to 2 ³⁄₄" x 1 ³⁄₄", with the design centered. Cut batting to the same size. Place the embroidered fabric right side on the batting, and baste around, close to the edges. Glue the batting to the frame back, inside the rope edging. Lay the mitered strips on top, covering the edges of the fabric. Glue the strips in place. ✤

Granny-Square Afghans & Pillows

shown on pages 88-89

Dimensions: Roses on Cream: Motif, 1¼" square; Afghan, 4" x 5", including ¼" edging all around; Pillow, 1¾" square, including ¼" ruffle all around. Roses on Black: Motif, 2" square; Afghan, 6½" x 8⅝", including edging all around; Pillow, 2½" square, including ⅜" ruffle all around

Materials & Tools

- Sewing and embroidery needles
- Steam iron

For Roses on Black Afghan
- Boye Steel Crochet Hook Size #11
- DMC Tatting Thread: 3 balls Black #310—background color (BC), 1 ball each Light Pink #818, Medium Pink #776, Dark Pink #899, and Mint Green #504

For Roses on Cream Afghan
- Boye Steel Crochet Hook Size #14
- DMC Machine Embroidery Thread, 1 spool each Cream #712-background color (BC), Light Pink #819, Medium Pink #818, Dark Pink #761, and Mint Green #710

For Pillows:
- Small amount of pink silk or satin fabric, for background and backing
- Sewing thread to match fabric
- 1 to 4 cotton balls, or small amount of fiberfill, for stuffing

Directions

Notes: Refer to page 72 for crochet abbreviations. Though you may prefer to vary the colors, use the type of thread and hook appropriate to the size afghan you are making.

How to Make a Tr Cluster: Holding back last 2 loops of tr, make 3 tr, then pull through all loops on hook: tr cluster made.

ROSE MOTIF:

Make 13: 12 for an afghan, one per pillow. Start at center of rose with dark pink and appropriate hook. Ch 4, sl st in first ch to form a ring.

Round 1: Ch 6 (first dc, ch 3), dc and ch 3 three times in ring, sl st into third ch of ch 6.

Round 2: Sl st into first sp, work sc, 3 dc, sc in same space. * Sc, 3 dc, sc, * repeat from * to * in each space all around; sl st into first sc.

Round 3: Ch 3, fold petals toward front of work. Holding petals down as you work, * sc through front and back of work above top of dc spoke made in round 1, ch 3, sc through front and back of second dc petal next to bottom of middle of petal. * Repeat from * to * all around; sl st into first sc (8 ch-3 loops made). Fasten off.

Round 4: With medium pink and with flower facing away from you (working on wrong side), sc, 4 dc, sc into first loop and in each loop around (8 petals made); sl st into first sc.

Round 5: Still working on wrong side, ch 1. Folding and holding petals away from you, sc around the post of sc in previous round, ch 4. Repeat all around (8 ch-4 loops made); sl st into first sc. Fasten off.

Round 6: With light pink (and still working on the wrong side), work sc, 5 dc, sc in first loop and in each loop all around; sl st into first sc (8 petals made).

Round 7: Repeat round 5; fasten off.

Round 8: On right side of work, attach mint green with sl st into first sc of previous round, ch 4, * 2 tr, 2 dc, 2 hdc, 1 sc, in loop, ch 3, skip sc. In next loop work 1 sc , 2 hdc, 2 dc, 2 tr, * 1 tr in next sc. Repeat from * to * all around, ending with sl st into top of ch-4. Fasten off.

Round 9: Holding fastening-off thread down, attach BC with sl st between ch 4 and first tr, ch 2, skip 2 tr, * sc between tr and dbl, ch 2, make tr cluster. Ch 2, tr cluster, ch 2, tr cluster, ch 2 in ch-3 loop, sc between next dc and next tr, ch 3, skip 1 tr, sc between next tr, ch 3. * Repeat from * to * all around; ch 1, hdc into first sc.

Round 10: In loop just formed ch 4, 2 tr, leaving 1 st of each on hook (makes 1 tr cluster). Ch 2, tr cluster, ch 2, tr cluster, ch 2, tr cluster (4 tr clusters in all), ch 3, * skip 1 cluster, sc in ch-2 space, ch 3, skip tr cluster, sc in ch-2 sp, ch 3, tr cluster, ch 2, tr cluster, ch 2, tr cluster, ch 4, tr cluster, ch 3, * repeat from * to * all around ending with ch 2. Sl st in top of ch 4 of beginning cluster.

Round 11: Sl st across to second cluster, * ch 2, sc in next cluster, tr, ch 1 (9 times) in ch 3 loop, ch 1, skip 1 cluster, sc in top of next cluster. * Repeat from * to * all around, ending with ch 1. Sl st into top of starting cluster.

Granny-Square Afghans & Pillows

continued

Round 12: Sl st into ch-2 sp, ch 3, 2 dc in ch-2 loop, 3 dc in each of the next 2 ch-1 spaces, skip ch-1 sp. In next tr make 3 dc, ch 2 , 3 dc, skip next ch-1 sp, 3 dc in each of the next 3 ch-1 spaces, skip 1 tr, 3 dc in next ch-1 sp, skip next tr, 3 dc in next ch-1 sp, skip next tr, 3 dc in next ch-1 sp. * Repeat from * to * all around, ending with sl st in top of ch 3. Fasten off.

Roses on Black Afghan

Assembly: Arrange 4 rows of 3 motifs each. Using matching sewing thread, whipstitch motifs in each row, then whipstitch rows together.

Edging: Sl st in any corner space. Ch 4, work 2 tr, ch 4, sl st in fourth chain from hook (picot made). Work 3 tr in same space, ch 5, skip 6 dc, sc in the space before the next dc, skip 6 dc, 3 tr, picot, 3 tr in the space before the next dc. Continue in this manner all around. End ch 5, sl st in top of first tr. Fasten off.

Finishing: Lay afghan right side down on a terrycloth towel. Lightly steam-press afghan from the back.

Roses on Cream Afghan

Assembly: Work same as for Roses on Black Afghan.

Edging: Sl st in any corner space, work ch 5. Tr and ch 1 five times, tr, skip 6 dc, sc in space before the next dc. Skip 6 dc; in space before the next dc work 7 tr with 1 ch in between. Continue in this manner all around. End with sl st in fourth ch of beginning ch- 5. Fasten off.

Finishing: See afghan above.

Pillow

Ruffle Edging:

Round 1: Continuing with BC, sl st into corner ch-2 space. Work ch 4, sc, ch 4, sc, ch 4, sc in same space, skip 3 dc, ch 4, sc, ch 4, sc, ch 4, sc in space between skipped 3 dc and next 3 dc, ch 4, skip 3 dc, sc, ch 4, sc in next space, ch 4, skip 3 dc, sc, ch 4, sc, ch 4, sc in next space. Ch 4, skip 3 dc. Continue all around, ending with ch 1, hdc in corner space.

Round 2: Ch 3, sc in next loop around, ending with ch 1, hdc in starting loop.

Round 3: Ch 3, sc in next loop around, ending with sl st into beginning loop. Fasten off.

Finishing: Measure the rose motif, excluding the ruffle edging. Cut 2 squares $\frac{1}{4}''$ larger all around than these measurements from pink fabric, for pillow background and backing. Pin fabric squares together with right sides facing, and stitch around 3 sides, $\frac{1}{4}''$ from raw edges and using matching sewing thread. Clip across seam allowances at corners and turn to right side. Stuff with cotton ball(s) or a bit of fiberfill. Turn in open edges; slip-stitch the pillow closed. Slip-stitch edges of rose motif to seams, allowing the crocheted ruffle edging to extend beyond the seams. ✿

Sweet Containers

Dimensions: Approximately 3″ high

Materials

- Small glass jars; these once held bouillon cubes and artichoke hearts
- ¾ yard of Offray sheer ribbon: wire-edge, ⅞″ wide in Light Coral, or Lady Chiffon Ultra Sheer, ⅝″ wide, in Pink
- Thick tacky glue
  For broad jar:
- 1 sheet Creative Gifted Sticker, "Roses For You" (same sheet is used for all vanity decoupage)
  For narrow jar:
- 1 package dried mini rosebuds

Directions

For Either Container: Wrap rim of jar with ribbon; tie a bow and notch the streamer ends.

For the Broad Jar: Apply stickers around the jar. Begin with the larger stickers, then fill in the spaces with the smaller stickers.

For the Narrow Jar: Remove the stems from the rosebuds. Apply glue to the side of each bud, and adhere to the wrapped ribbon. Apply glue to the base of 3 buds, and adhere to the bow knot. (*Note:* You may wish to substitute hot glue for this procedure, but not if the jar is to contain a lit votive candle which would cause hot glue to melt.) ⚘

MATCHBOX VANITY

Dimensions: Vanity, 5″ by 2½″ by 2¾″ high; Stool, 2″ in diameter and 2″ high

Materials & Tools

- ⚘ 11 Diamond matchboxes (empty)
- ⚘ ⅜ yard Lion Moire ribbon, 1½″ wide, in Celadon
- ⚘ ¼ yard emerald green moire fabric, 45″ wide
- ⚘ ¾ yard ivory passementerie (upholstery) trim, ⅜″ wide
- ⚘ 1 sheet Creative Gifted Sticker ("Roses For You")
- ⚘ 10 gold 6mm jump rings
- ⚘ 10 gold 3mm beads
- ⚘ 2 gold bead caps
- ⚘ 2 gold bola tips
- ⚘ 2 flat gold ⁷⁄₁₆″ squares; these are earring dangles
- ⚘ Matboard

- ⚘ 1 jar facial skin cream; used here: Mary Kay Skin Revival Cream
- ⚘ 1 miniature vanity mirror
- ⚘ Gold paint pen
- ⚘ Dark green sewing thread
- ⚘ Tacky craft glue
- ⚘ Scissors
- ⚘ Needlenose pliers
- ⚘ Hot glue gun and glue stick
- ⚘ Toothpicks
- ⚘ Sewing needle or sewing machine
- ⚘ Iron

Directions

Vanity Assembly: Remove matchboxes from their covers. To create the gilded edges of the drawer fronts, use a gold paint pen to mark the edges of 10 covers at one end. Allow to dry. Create the chest of drawers by stacking two sets of 5 matchbox covers, making sure the gilded edges all face forward, and the striking surfaces are in a line. Glue each set together using tacky craft glue.

To cover the sides of each stacked set, cut matboard into 4 rectangles 2″ x 2⅝″, or sized to cover. For the vanity top, cut a 2¼″ x 4¾″ rectangle. Cut a fabric piece, ¼″ larger all around, for each matboard piece. Spread a thin layer of tacky glue on the wrong side of fabric. Center, adhere each matboard piece to its corresponding fabric piece, and wrap the fabric edges over to the reverse side of the matboard. Glue the 4 identical fabric-covered matboard pieces to the sides of the stacked sets, aligning the outside edges. Glue the vanity top across the top of the two stacks, aligning the outside edges. Allow to dry.

Making a Skirt: Cut a 3″ x 27″ strip of emerald fabric. Turn all edges ¼″ to the wrong side, and stitch to hem. Gather one long edge. Adjust the gathers to fit around the sides and back of vanity, and hot-glue in place, distributing the gathers evenly as you glue. Hot-glue upholstery trim all around the vanity's top surface.

Covering the Drawer Fronts: Cut and glue celadon ribbon to cover one end of each matchbox. Accent the top, bottom, and middle drawer fronts of each stack with pieces cut from the sticker border. Create each drawer pull by opening a jump ring, using needlenose pliers. Place a gold bead in the opening and close the ring with pliers. Glue the bead to the center of each drawer front, using a toothpick to apply tacky glue.

Matchbox Vanity

continued

Note: Drawer pulls are decorative, not functional. To open the drawers, push the matchbox from the back.

Vanity Mirror Stand: Using a paint pen, gild the ends of the remaining matchbox, and the outside edges of the matchbox cover. Glue ribbon around the matchbox cover. Decorate this mirror stand with pieces cut from the sticker border. Place in the center of vanity.

Creating Table Lamps: Hot-glue a square earring dangle and a bead cap to opposite ends of a bola. Hot-glue the lamp on the vanity top to secure.

Make the Stool: Glue ribbon over the lid of the face cream jar, trimming and notching ribbon to lay flat. For a skirt, measure the jar; from fabric, cut a strip $\frac{1}{2}''$ longer than the height of the jar, and equal in length to 3 times the circumference of the jar. Fold the strip crosswise in half, with right sides facing, and stitch along the ends, to form a ring. Turn the long edges $\frac{1}{4}''$ to the wrong side, and stitch to hem. Press. Gather the ribbon along one hemmed edge. Adjust these gathers to fit around the jar lid, and hot-glue them flush with the top edge of the lid. Hot-glue upholstery trim around the top, and apply a sticker to the center of the seat. ⬦

Stenciled Floorcloth

Dimensions: 4″ x 6″

Materials & Tools

- 𝄢 *4″ x 6″ piece of Kreative Kanvas from Kunin Felt*
- 𝄢 *DecoArt Americana acrylic paint in Buttermilk (DA3), French Mauve (DA186), Green Mist (DA177), Golden Straw (DA168), and Raspberry (DA28)*
- 𝄢 *DecoArt Matte Varnish*

- 𝄢 *Pencil, ruler*
- 𝄢 *Paintbrushes: 1″ flat, $\frac{1}{4}''$ flat*
- 𝄢 *4 stencil brushes, $\frac{3}{16}''$ diameter*
- 𝄢 *American Traditional Stencils: Ivy & Victorian, MS-216; and Victorian Corner, MS-9*
- 𝄢 *Low-tack masking tape*
- 𝄢 *Paper towels*

Directions

Preparation: Paint one side of the canvas with two coats of Buttermilk paint, allowing it to dry after each coat. Pencil a $2\frac{3}{8}''$ x $4\frac{3}{8}''$ rectangle in the center. Apply tape and paint inside the rectangle with French Mauve. Allow to dry. Use tape to enable you to paint a $\frac{1}{8}''$ band of Green Mist around the outer edges and around the center rectangle. Allow to dry.

Stenciling: Read the "Stenciling Know-How," on page 50. Center the Victorian edge (Ivy & Victorian) along one short side of the canvas. Refer to the photograph for suggested colors and positioning, and stencil as directed in the Stenciling Know-How. In the same manner, stencil the opposite side, and stencil two motifs on each long side. Stencil a single motif in each corner. On the mauve rectangle, stencil a large triangular shaped motif (Victorian Corner) in each corner. Stencil a single "star" motif (Victorian Corner) at the center of the rug. Allow to dry for 24 hours.

Finishing: Apply 2 to 3 coats of varnish, allowing to dry between coats. ⬦

Victorian Parlor

Seating: Sofa, Armchair, Slipper Chair

Dimensions: Sofa, 5″ wide by 2¼″ deep by 3″ high; armchair, 2⅞″ wide by 2¼″ deep by 3″ high; slipper (armless) chair, 2″ wide by 2¼ deep by 3″ high

Materials & Tools

- Sculpey III modeling compound (from Polyform, and hereafter referred to as "clay") in 2-ounce packages: 3 teal, 1 maroon
- Balsa wood sheet ⅜″ thick, 3″ x 36″
- Flathead nails, ¾″
- 12 gold beads, 5mm
- 1 yard of gold guimpe, braid, or trim, ¾″ wide
- ½ yard of twisted gold cord, ⅛″ thick
- 6 gold seed beads
- White craft glue
- Rolling pin
- Craft knife and utility knife with sharp blades
- T-square
- Small rubber stamp of snowflake or flower
- Rubber-tipped tools for working with polymer clay, such as Colour Shapers
- Wood skewer, toothpick
- Fine woven fabric
- Oven
- Cookie sheet, oven mitts, spatula

Directions

Constructing Foundations: Working on a protected surface and using a sharp utility knife and T-square, mark and cut the following rectangles from balsa wood: For the sofa, two 4½″ x 1⅜″ (A), one 4½″ x 2¼″ (B), and one 4½″ x 1¾″ (C). For the armchair, two 2″ x 1½″ (A), one 2″ x 2¼″ (B), and one 1⅞″ x 2″ (C). For the slipper chair, two 1⅜″ x 1¾″ (A), one 1¾″ x 2¼″ (B), and one 1¾″ x 1¾″ (C).

Glue the balsa pieces together as follows: For the seat, glue the two A pieces together to make a single, solid block. When the glue is dry, use a utility knife to shave along he back edge of the top A

piece so that it tapers down just a bit. This will form the crevice between the seat and the sofa/chair back. For the sofa back, use B, and shave one 4 ½″ edge so that the top will be slightly rounded. Do the same with one 2″ edge of the armchair's B piece, and one 1¾″ edge of the slipper chair's B piece. Glue piece B to the back edge of the joined A block, referring to the diagram, which shows the sofa foundation as seen from the bottom. Glue piece C to the bottom of the furniture, covering A and the bottom edge of B.

Thread gold beads onto small flathead nails, and push the nails into the bottom of each sofa or chair at the corners, for ball feet.

Covering the Foundations: Read "Working with Polymer Clay," on page 18. Begin with teal clay, and smooth a small wad onto the seat so that it will be raised in the center. For the sofa, use a 3½″ x ½″ sausage roll; for each chair, use a ¾″ ball.

DIAGRAM FOR THE FOUNDATION

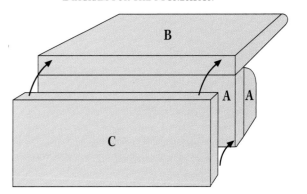

VICTORIAN PARLOR
continued

Roll out a large, $\frac{1}{8}''$ thick sheet of teal clay and lightly press a flower-shaped rubber stamp into the clay for an all-over texture. Cut a rectangle of clay big enough to fit over the seat of the balsa foundation and extend slightly over the front and side edges. Lay the sheet onto the chair seat, and gently pat the clay down onto the center of the seat without disturbing the impressed pattern. Use your fingers to push the edges of the clay sheet down firmly onto the balsa for good adhesion.

Next, cut a sheet of clay large enough to cover the sofa or chair back, wrapping from the seat, just over the top of the sofa or chair back, and wide enough to wrap around the sides. Press the clay firmly in place. Pinch the clay together to flatten the top corners. Cut a piece of clay to cover the very back of the sofa/chair and overlap the previously applied clay pieces. Smooth gently with a rubber-tipped tool where the clay overlaps. Also use this tool to close the gaps in the clay, particularly in the crevice where the chair back and seat meet. Use a rubber stamp to maintain the patterned texture.

Creating Arms (omit for slipper chair): Add $\frac{5}{8}''$ rolls of clay that are $1\frac{1}{4}''$ long. Attach them so that the roll extends slightly beyond the front edge of the chair seat. Lay a $1\frac{3}{4}'' \times 1\frac{1}{2}''$ sheet of textured teal clay over the roll and work the clay gently around the roll of clay with a rubber-tipped tool. Make a tiny circle of clay to put over the front end. Make creases in the clay with a toothpick to simulate pleats in upholstery fabric.

Adding a Draped Back: Roll out maroon clay into a thin sheet. Give the surface of the clay a texture by using a rolling pin to firmly press fabric with a fine woven texture into the clay. Remove the fabric. Cut a piece of maroon clay that will cover the headrest section of the back of the chair; round the corners. Lay it onto the chair back and gently attach the edges with a rubber-tipped tool. Use a rubber chisel to depress staggered rows of U-shaped marks into the draped clay, to simulate tufted upholstery. (Note: You may also make a tool to leave a similar pattern by rolling a cardboard cylinder with a $\frac{1}{4}''$ diameter, and clipping away the cardboard at one end, leaving a semi-circular edge.) Lay a piece of narrow cording along the edge of the drape, and push it firmly into the clay with the flat end of a wood skewer.

Making the Skirt: Roll a thin sheet of maroon clay and cut a $1\frac{1}{8}''$ wide strip, long enough to wrap around each seating piece. Overlap the teal clay with this strip, pressing for good adhesion and making an invisible seam where the ends meet. Stretch the long bottom edge to create an undulating or ruffled effect.

Creating Little Tassels: For each tassel, roll a tiny sausage of clay. Push a seed bead into the top of the roll of clay. Roll a toothpick around the seed bead to create the "neck" of the tassel. Use a craft knife to make 6 or 8 lengthwise cuts into the section of the sausage below the neck, for streamer ends. Poke tiny holes along the neck of the tassel. Press a tassel onto the ends of the draped back cord, and onto the front of the arms.

Baking: Place each piece of furniture on a cookie sheet in a pre-heated, 275° oven for 20 minutes. Let cool. Glue gold trim around the piece, $\frac{1}{8}''$ below the top edge of the skirt.

HEXAGONAL TABLE

Dimensions: $2\frac{1}{2}''$ across and $1\frac{5}{8}''$ high

Materials & Tools

- *2 packages of Chocolate-colored Sculpey III (from Polyform, and hereafter referred to as "clay")*
- *6 each: gold seed beads and gold glass pebble beads, from Mill Hill*
- *Clear acrylic finish*
- *Epoxy or strong adhesive, such as Goop*
- *Rubber stamps: patchwork or mosaic geometric, approximately 1" square, and small snowflake or flower, approximately $\frac{1}{2}''$ across*
- *Same tools as for Sofa and Chairs*

Directions

Making the Side Panels: Working on a protected surface, roll out clay into a $\frac{1}{8}''$ sheet. Use a utility knife to cut out six $1\frac{1}{4}''$ squares. Use a rubber stamp to impress a geometric pattern over each square. For the table shown here, 2 different stamps were used together to produce a complex pattern. After stamping, re-cut the squares so they again measure exactly 1¼" on each side, but cut the side edges on a slight angle, so the back surface measures only 1" across. Join the 6 squares to make a hexagonal box (open at top and bottom), with the patterned side out. Make snakes to cover each seam on the inside. Repeat on the outside, but use very slender snakes, and with a toothpick, press fine lines across each of these snakes.

Making the Tabletop: Lay the box on an ⅛" sheet of clay, and lightly trace the outer edges of the box. Use a ruler and craft knife to cut out a hexagon ¼" larger all around than the traced outline. Lightly incise lines across the tabletop connecting the corners. Stamp a small design in the center. Press a seed bead into the edge at each corner. Center the tabletop over the hexagonal box. Use a rubber-tipped tool to smooth the top edges of each panel and the ends of the inside snakes onto the underside of the tabletop.

Finishing: Bake the table, following the clay manufacturer's instructions. Let cool. If desired, apply an clear acrylic finish. Glue a pebble bead to the bottom of each corner of the box, for ball feet.

Occasional Table

Dimensions: 1" by 1⅜" by 2⅛" high

Materials & Tools

- *Chocolate Sculpey III modeling compound (from Polyform; hereafter referred to as "clay"), one 2-ounce package*
- *7 gold seed beads*
- *3 gold bugle beads, ½"*
- *White craft glue*
- *Acrylic varnish (optional)*
- *Same tools as for Sofa and Chairs*

Directions

Making the Tabletop: Roll out a thin sheet of clay. Cut a rectangle 1¼" x ⅞". Cut a strip of clay ⅛" wide

and wrap it around the rectangle like a frame. With the tip of a toothpick, make depressions along the sides of the frame. Push a gold seed bead into each corner. Set on cookie sheet.

Build the Legs: Roll 3 snakes each ¼" thick and 2¼" long. Join the 3 snakes together at one end (the top) and slice off ⅛" at this end to make it perfectly flat. Stand the 3 legs up on the flat end and wedge a tiny ball of clay in between the 3 legs, for solidity. Push a bugle bead into each crease between adjacent legs at the top end.

Slice ⅛" off the bottom of each of the 3 legs, and splay the legs slightly, as shown in the photograph. Push a gold seed bead into the bottom of each leg. Arrange the legs on a cookie sheet in the upright position in which they will be used.

Finishing: Bake the 2 parts for 15 minutes in a 275° oven. When cool, glue the top to the legs. Give the table a coat of acrylic varnish if a gloss or sheen is desired.

Potted Plants

Dimensions: Pot, approximately 1" in diameter at the top; potted plant, about 2½" high

Materials & Tools

- *Black Sculpey III modeling compound (hereafter referred to as "clay") in 2-ounce package*

For Large Plant:

- *Gold Rub 'n Buff (or acrylic paint)*
- *Green florist's tape, 1" wide*
- *Fine florist's wire*
- *White craft glue*
- *Thimble*
- *Cellophane wrap*
- *Cookie sheet, spatula, oven mitt*
- *Oven*

For Small Plant:

- *Cap from glue or toothpaste*
- *Sprig of air fern*

continued

Directions

Preparing Containers: For a large plant, roll clay to an ⅛" thickness. Wrap a thimble in cellophane, then cover the bottom and sides with pieces of clay. Seal the edges of the clay. Gently pull out cellophane-wrapped thimble. Wrap a thin snake of clay around the top edge of the clay container, for a rim. Bake on a cookie sheet, following the manufacturer's instructions. Let cool, then gild the rim with gold Rub 'n Buff or paint. For a small plant, use a cap from glue or toothpaste.

Adding the Plant: For a small container, wrap the bottom of a sprig of air fern with clay, and push gently into the container. (Do not bake.)

For the large palm, make 8 fronds as follows: Cut one piece of florist's tape 2" to 3" in length. Lay it on a protected work surface, wrong side up. Cover this side completely with a thin layer of glue. Place a piece of wire down the center of the tape, starting ¼" from one end and extending 1" beyond the other end, for a stem. Press a second piece of same-size tape firmly over the glued tape, encasing the wire. Wipe away any excess glue and allow the tape to dry. Following the diagram, round the tape to form a broad, tapered leaf (you may stop there for a corn-plant, lily, or aspidistra plant); then cut "teeth" into the leaf as shown. Bend the wire to curve the frond gracefully. Stroke the "teeth" to hang downwards. Fill the container with a ball of clay, and push the stem ends into the center. ◊

DIAGRAM FOR A PALM FROND

Fireplace Bookend

Dimensions: 9" across at base by 3" deep by 11" high

Materials & Tools

- ❧ *Styrofoam brand plastic foam sheet, 1" x 12" x 8"*
- ❧ *8-ounce can of acrylic spackle medium (Onetime Spackling compound by Red Devil was used here)*
- ❧ *Small stones*
- ❧ *Acrylic paints: dark brown, burnt sienna, black, pewter*
- ❧ *Small amount of clean sand*
- ❧ *Matboard*
- ❧ *Balsa wood, 5mm x 2⅛" x 7½"*
- ❧ *13" length of (mini) decorative wood trim, 5mm*
- ❧ *Simple metal bookend standard*
- ❧ *Brown velour fabric or felt, for backing*
- ❧ *White craft glue*
- ❧ *2 mini clothespins*
- ❧ *Wooden craft (Popsicle) stick*

- *Pieces of artificial evergreen*
- *Scrap of red ribbon, ¼″ wide*
- *Two 1″ candy canes*
- *Miniature Christmas "lights"; shown here is from a packet of 30 bulbs 5mm × 8mm, from Darice*
- *Floral adhesive (putty)*
- *Graph paper*
- *Pencil*
- *Ruler, T-square, or clear quilter's ruler*
- *Craft knife with a sharp blade*
- *Small putty knife*
- *Saw*
- *Disposable container, such as a large plastic yogurt container*
- *Soft paintbrush*
- *Clean rags*
- *Hot glue gun and glue sticks*

Directions

Making the Foundation: Follow the diagrams below to draw actual-size patterns for the Front Section and Back Section, and for the Mantel on graph paper, or enlarge the diagram on a photocopier until the dimensions measure as indicated. Use the patterns to cut one Front and one Back Section from plastic foam. Hot-glue the Front Section onto the Back Section, aligning bottom and side edges.

Stonework: Mix a bit more than half the jar of spackle with a small amount of brown paint and about 5 tablespoons of clean sand. Stir until everything is well mixed. Keep the container holding this "mortar" covered at all times to prevent the surface from drying out. Pick through the stones and select flat, broad ones as much as possible.

Place the fireplace foundation flat on newspaper. Spread a ¼″ thick layer of the mortar onto one side surface of the fire chamber. Push stones directly into the mortar and even into the surface of the plastic foam to a slight degree. Try to leave as little space between stones as possible. Sometimes the mortar bulges up around the stone as you push the stone. Tap this bump down gently with your fingertip or use a soft brush to even out the mortar.

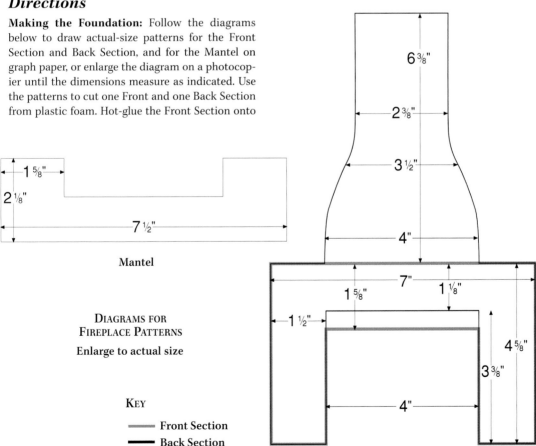

Mantel

DIAGRAMS FOR
FIREPLACE PATTERNS

Enlarge to actual size

KEY

Front Section
Back Section

FIREPLACE BOOKEND
continued

Continue to cover each surface of the fireplace, working on a small area at a time, and proceeding in this order: inside surfaces, sides, then front. Leave a 1/4" space uncovered around the base of the chimney at the mantel line for the balsa and decorative wood trim. Build up a 1/4" edge of mortar around the very top of the chimney. Cut matboard 9" x 3" and 5½" x 4". Spread a very thin layer of mortar over the front of the 5½" x 4" rectangle, for the back of the fire chamber.

Before setting the fireplace aside to dry, make sure that no mortar extends above the mantel line or below the base line. Check this by setting a straight edge across the uncovered sections; use a brush to remove any excess mortar.

Making the Hearth: Score the 9" x 3" matboard into ½" squares, using the craft knife and a T-square, or clear quilter's ruler. Use a rag to rub on burnt sienna paint to simulate terra cotta tile. Let dry.

Making the Mantel: Use the actual-size pattern to cut the mantel from 5mm balsa; use a sharp craft knife and a T-square or ruler, and work on a protected surface. Cut a length of decorative wood trim into two pieces each 2⅛" long, and one piece 8" long. Glue the trim onto the edges of the mantel, sides first, then across the front. When the glue is dry, stain the mantel: rub on brown paint thinned with a little water; immediately wipe off the excess with a rag.

Assembly: Use white craft glue to glue the mantel on the fireplace. Use hot glue to glue the tile hearth onto the bottom of the fireplace. Glue the back of the fire chamber so that it fits snugly on the tile hearth. Glue the entire fireplace onto a bookend, using a generous amount of hot glue. Use the entire pattern, ignoring the fireplace opening, to cut a backing just ⅛" smaller all around, from velour fabric or felt. Use hot glue to adhere this backing behind the fireplace and chimney, encasing the metal bookend upright.

Filling the Fireplace: Use thinned black paint and an almost dry brush to darken the inside of the fire chamber and make it look as if the fireplace has been well-used. For andirons, saw the leg ends from 2 mini clothespins, leaving a ½" slit. Cut two 1½" lengths from a craft stick, and insert one end of each

stick into the slit of a clothespin. Glue to secure. Paint the andirons black, and rub in a bit of pewter or gray paint to highlight and "antique" them. Hot-glue the andirons in the fire chamber, then hot-glue a few 2" to 3" sticks in a stack that spans the andirons.

Decorating for Christmas: For a wreath, cut a 6½" length of artficial evergreen and twist the ends together for ¼" to form a ring. At the join, hot-glue a ribbon bow, catching 2 mini candy canes under the knot. Use floral adhesive to attach the wreath temporarily to the chimney. For a garland, cut pieces of artificial evergreen and twist the ends together to obtain a total 12" length. Wrap mini Christmas lights along the length. Bend the garland so it follows the contours of the mantel top. Secure this, the stockings, and any other accessories in place with floral adhesive. ✧

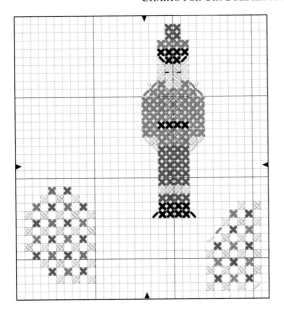
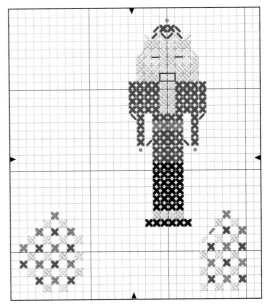

KEY

Cross Stitch and Half Cross Stitch
DMC Rayon Floss unless otherwise indicated
- **✖** Black #30310
- **✖** Red #30349
- **✖** Royal Blue #30797
- ✖ Ecru #30746
- ✖ Gold Metallic Floss #5282

Backstitch
- ⬗ Gold Metallic Floss #5282
- — Black Rayon Floss #30310

Bead Work
- ● Red #42013
- ○ Gold #40557

TIN SOLDIER AND NUTCRACKER STOCKINGS

Dimensions: 2¼″ long

Materials & Tools

- ✿ Small amount of Zweigart white Hardanger even-weave fabric, 22-count
- ✿ DMC Rayon Floss, 1 skein of each color listed in the key
- ✿ DMC Gold Metallic Floss
- ✿ Mill Hill Petite Glass Beads in Red Red #42013 and Gold #40557
- ✿ Thin, fusible interfacing
- ✿ Red and white sewing thread
- ✿ Scraps of ribbons, ³/₈″ wide and ¹/₈″ wide
- ✿ Embroidery, beading and sewing needles
- ✿ Pins
- ✿ Sewing machine
- ✿ Embroidery hoop
- ✿ Iron
- ✿ Tracing paper and pencil
- ✿ Sewing machine
- ✿ Optional: magnifier

Directions

Preparation: Read "How to Cross Stitch" on page 125.
Stitching: Use 2 strands of rayon floss or 1 strand of metallic floss, and work over 1 thread throughout. Following the chart and key, work all cross stitches, then half cross stitches, then backstitches.

117

STOCKINGS
continued

Beadwork: Use a beading needle and sew on each bead separately with one strand of white sewing thread. For durability, pass through each bead twice with the needle and thread.

Assembly: Fuse interfacing to the back of the cross stitch, and to the remaining fabric, for backing. Trace the actual-size stocking pattern onto tracing paper, and position it over the cross-stitch design, aligning the heel and toe areas, and centering the figure. Pin the pattern in place, and cut out along the marked pattern lines.

Pin the cross-stitched front on interfaced fabric for backing, with wrong sides together. Using white thread, machine-stitch around the stocking front, 1/8″ from the edges, leaving the top edge unstitched. Cut the backing to the same size as the front. Using red thread, make decorative stitches along the previous stitches and over the edges: make zigzag or buttonhole stitches by machine, or tiny blanket or overcast stitches by hand.

For a hanging loop, cut a 2″ length of 1/8″ wide ribbon. Fold it in half, and insert the ends into the stocking so a 1/2″ loop extends from the top above the heel. Pin 3/8″ wide ribbon around the top, extending slightly beyond the cut edge; turn the ends under neatly at the seam above the heel. Take tiny slip-stitches to secure this trim in place. Fill the stocking with miniature Christmas items or other lightweight goodies. ⬦

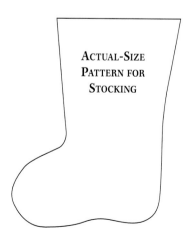

ACTUAL-SIZE
PATTERN FOR
STOCKING

Knit Abbreviations

beg	–	beginning
CC	–	contrast color thread
dec	–	decrease
inc	–	increase
k	–	knit
MC	–	main color thread
p	–	purl
psso	–	pass slip stitch over (psso 2 means pass 2 slip stitches over)
st	–	stitch
st st	–	stockinette stitch (knit one row, purl one row)
tog	–	together
( )	–	repeat directions in parentheses as indicated following the closed parentheses

ELVES' CLOTHING

Dimensions: To fit a medium-sized elf, 5″ tall

Materials & Tools

- ❦ J. & P. Coats Knit-Cro-Sheen, article A-64 (150-yard balls): 1 ball Spanish Red #126; 1 ball White #1, from Coats & Clark
- ❦ Coats & Clark Southmaid Crochet Cotton, article D-54 (350-yard ball): 1 ball Myrtle Green #484
- ❦ J. & P. Coats Metallic Knit-Cro-Sheen (100-yard ball): 1 ball Gold #9OG
- ❦ Red, white, and green sewing thread
- ❦ 1/4″ gold-toned jingle bells: 1 for each hat and 1 for each shoe
- ❦ Mill Hill Glass Seed Beads, Gold #02011
- ❦ Knitting needles size 1 or size needed to obtain required gauge
- ❦ Small safety pins for stitch holders

Directions

Gauge: 9 sts and 13 rows = 1″ with size 1 needles over st st

Colors: For one outfit, MC is Spanish Red; CC is Myrtle Green; for the other outfit, MC is Myrtle Green and CC is Spanish Red.

Finishing Notes: Because these garments are so tiny, weaving loose ends into the garment itself would make the seams too bulky. Instead, tie off and knot loose ends, snip them to ¹/₂″. Then, with a sewing needle and sewing thread to match the garment, whipstitch along the inside of the garment, catching the loose ends and anchoring them neatly to the knitted surface. The loose ends for the boots, stockings, and mittens can simply be pushed down into the item where they will not show.

HAT

With CC, cast on 24 sts. K 2 rows with CC. K 2 rows with gold. K 4 rows with CC. Brim is now finished. Work now in st st (k 1 row, p 1 row), working in stripe pattern as follows: (2 rows MC; 2 rows CC). After first 4 rows of st st are worked, keep to stripe sequence as established. At the same time, dec 1 st at beg and end of every k row until 2 sts remain. P back across these 2 sts. Break off thread, leaving a long tail. Weave thread through last 2 sts, pull tightly, and fasten securely. Sew back seam. Sew jingle bell to tip of hat.

SHIRT

Beg at back, with CC, cast on 26 sts. Change to gold and K 2 rows. Change to CC and K 2 rows.

Change to white. Work now in st st (k 1 row, p 1 row) until there are a total of 18 st st rows.

Shoulder Shaping: (K 2 tog) 5 times, k 6, (k 2 tog) 5 times. P back over 16 sts.

Shoulders and Neck: Change to CC. K 2 rows. Change to gold. K 2 rows. Change to CC. K 1 row. On next row, k 5, bind off center 6 sts, k 5. Fasten off CC.

Right Front: Change to white. K 2 into first 5 sts. Continue in st st over 10 sts until there are a total of 8 rows from shoulder. Work Left Front same as Right Front. Cast on 6 sts between left and right for center front. Work in st st over these 26 sts until there are a total of 20 st st rows from shoulder. Change to CC. K 2 rows. Change to gold. K 2 rows. Change to CC. K 1 row. Bind off all sts in k.

Sleeves: Mark 8 white rows down from each shoulder. With white, pick up and k 19 sts between markers. Work in st st until there are a total of 12 rows. Change to CC. (K 2 tog) across, ending k 1. K back across 10 sts. Change to gold. K 2 rows. Change to CC. K 1 row. Bind off all sts in k.

Finishing: Sew sleeve and body side seams. Front Plackets: with CC, pick up and k 6 sts along each side of front neck. K 2 rows. Bind off in k. Sew bottoms of plackets to cast-on white edge at center front. Sew a gold bead at each wrist seam. Sew 3 gold beads on each side of placket.

KNICKERS (Make 2, for Front and Back)

With MC, cast on 16 sts. Change to gold. K 2 rows with gold. Change to MC. K 2 rows. Inc Row: K 2 into each st across. P back across 32 sts. Work now in st st (k 1 row, p 1 row) evenly until there are a total of 14 st st rows.

Crotch Shaping: Bind off 5 sts at beg of next 2 rows. Dec 1 st at both ends of every other row 3 times. Work even over remaining 16 sts until there are a total of 10 st st rows from crotch shaping.

Casing: P 2 rows. Work in st st for 4 more rows. Bind off in k.

Sew leg seams. Sew sides tog at crotch. Turn casing to inside and sew down. Sew a gold bead at center of each bottom leg cuff.

MITTENS

With MC, cast on 12 sts. K 2 rows with MC. Change to gold. K 2 rows with gold. Change to MC.

ELVES' CLOTHING
continued

K 4 rows with MC. Change to CC. On first st st row, k 5, (k 2 into next st) twice, k 5. P back 14 sts. Change to MC. K 5, k 2 into next st, k 2, k 2 into next st, k 5. P back across 16 sts. Change to MC. K first 6 sts, cast on 2 sts, slip next 4 sts onto a pin for thumb, k across remaining 6 sts. P back across 14 sts. There are now 14 hand sts. Work in st st stripe pattern as established for 6 more rows. Dec at tip as follows: (k 2 tog) across. P back across 7 sts. Break off thread, leaving a long tail. Weave tail through remaining 7 sts and gather. Fasten securely.

Thumb: Sl 4 sts from pin onto needle. With MC, k 2 into first st, k 2, k 2 into last st. P back over 6 sts. Work 2 more rows st st with MC (thumb is not striped). K 2 tog across. Break off thread, leaving a long tail. Weave thread through remaining 3 sts and gather. Fasten securely. Sew thumb seam and sew thumb to hand at cast-on sts. Sew mitten side seam.

BOOTS

With CC, cast on 9 sts. K 2 rows. Cast on 6 sts at right of work. K 3 rows over 15 sts. K first 9 sts, bind off remaining 6.

Other Side of Foot: With CC, pick up and k 9 sts along cast-on edge. K 2 rows. Pick up and k 6 sts along cast-on edge. K 2 rows. Bind off 6 sts at beginning of next row, k across remaining 9 sts.

Join at Top: K 8, k last st from this side of foot and first st from other side tog, k 8. K 8, k 2 tog, k 7. K 7, k 2 tog, k 7-15 sts. K back across these sts.

The top of boot is now divided into five 3-st sections. The 1st, 3rd, and 5th section are worked with MC, the 2nd and 4th are worked with CC. For all sections: K 4 rows. Sl 2, k 1, psso 2. Fasten off securely.

Finishing: Sew inc sts at toe tog at top tightly; the more tightly sewn the seam, the more the toe will curl. Carefully weave loose ends from tips of sections to inside of boot. Sew back boot seam. Gather "ankle" with CC just at section's beginning. *Note:* Sections should curl out over top of boot. Sew a bell to tip of toe. Sew a gold bead on tip of each section.

STOCKINGS

With CC, cast on 16 sts. K 4 rows. Change to MC. Work in st st for 12 rows. Shape heels as follows:

With CC, work across first 4 sts, turn. P 2 tog, p 2, turn. K 3, turn. P 2 tog, p 1. Change to MC. K 2 tog, pick up and k 3 along the side of CC heel, k across until last 4 sts. Change to CC. K 4, turn. P 2, p 2 tog, turn. K 3, turn. P 1, p 2 tog. Break off CC. K 2 tog with MC, pick up and k 3 sts along side of CC heel—there are now 16 sts on needle.

Dec Row: P 3, p 2 tog, p 6, p 2 tog, p 3—14 sts on needle. Continue in MC st st until there are a total of 8 st st rows from heel. Break off MC.

Toes: With CC, k 2 tog, k 3, (k 2 tog) twice, k 3, k 2 tog. P back over 10 sts. K 2 tog, k 1, (k 2 tog) twice, k 1, k 2 tog. P back over 6 sts. Divide sts in half. K sts tog on wrong side. Sew foot and back seams. ♢

SUMMER CENTERPIECE: WOODLAND GAZEBO

Dimensions: About 6″ high; base is a 5″ × 6″ oval

Materials & Tools

- Styrofoam brand plastic foam: disc, 3″ in diameter and 1″ thick; block, 12″ x 12″ x ½″ thick; egg, 4½″ x 3 ½″
- Twigs, ⅛″ to ¼″ thick; **Note:** Always ask permission before taking plant materials from public or private property
- Aleene's Thick Designer Tacky Glue
- Forster craft (Popsicle) sticks
- Granitex stone-colored modeling compound in Black #3007
- ½ cup fine sawdust
- Plaid Folk Art Acrylic Color, 1 bottle each Emerald #647 and Clover #923
- Plaid Apple Barrel Colors Acrylic Craft Paint in Nutmeg Brown
- Small amount of brown twisted paper; used here: Maxwell-Wellington Floral Dec Wire Ties #M4308, ⅛″
- Green floral wire, 32 gauge
- Mill Hill beads, 1 package each: Seed Beads in Iris #00252; Antique Glass Seed Beads in Purple Passion #03053; Petite Glass Seed Beads in Iris #40252
- DMC embroidery floss in green #319
- Regenboog Dried Flowers: 1 package Plumosus #2991, for ferns on ground, 1 package Ming Fern #196152, for vine
- Kunin Felt: 9″ x 12″ sheet Kelly Green
- Creative Beginnings sun face #994616, or other charm to decorate top of gazebo
- 3 coral feather butterflies, ¾″
- Utility knife
- Clippers for cutting twigs and wire
- Paintbrushes
- Containers for mixing paint
- Beading needle
- Metal skewer

Directions

Cutting Twigs: Work on a cutting board or a protected surface. Use clippers or a utility knife. Cut as you go along, just until you have enough lengths to accomplish the task at hand.

Beginning the Gazebo Platform: Begin by cutting the thinnest sticks (⅛″ in diameter or less) into 1″ lengths. Glue these closely together around the edges of the plastic foam disk. Let dry. Glue another layer of sticks on top of the first layer, and let dry.

For the base of the centerpiece, cut a 5″ x 6″ oval from the plastic foam block. Center the platform on the back of the base; trace around it and cut a circle out of the base. Gently push the platform into the base, gluing around the bottom edges to secure.

Making Roof Supports (Columns): Cut eight 3″ lengths from twigs (these branch off with a Y fork or a trident at one end). Push these into the platform at regularly spaced intervals, with forks at the top.

Installing Flooring: Cut craft sticks to fit along top of platform, working around columns. Glue down to form a planked floor. Dilute brown paint with a little water and brush this mixture over the floor for a "stain." From ¼″ twigs, cut 7 baseboards each 1⅜″ in length, cutting ends on an angle. Glue baseboards around platform beyond columns, leaving one space between columns empty for a doorway. Cut thin twigs for crossbars to extend from column to column. Glue these ⅝″ above the floor, leaving the doorway open.

Roofing: Cut across the wider end of the plastic foam egg so that the flat edge is about 3″ in diameter. Paint the egg on all sides with undiluted brown paint. Let dry. Cut twigs 4″ long, and glue them over the egg to form a cone-shaped roof. To maintain the cone, make some sticks shorter, and use these to fill in the gaps between the first twigs. In the same manner, add one or two more layers of twigs, concealing the plastic foam completely. Paint tops of columns with a contrast color paint; carefully center the roof over the platform until the columns' twig tops touch the roof. Use a skewer to poke "pilot" holes into the roof at paint marks. Insert glue into these holes, and realign roof and platform. Carefully push tops of twigs into the underside of the roof. Let dry.

Making the Steps: Roll polymer clay out to a ¼″ thickness. Cut rectangles: 1⅛″ x 1″, 1⅛″ x ¾″, and 1⅛″ x ½″. Stack rectangles to form 3 steps. Smooth joins, and bake according to the manufacturer's instructions. Let cool, and position under doorway, but do not glue down at this time. Cut thin twigs for railing supports: two 1⅜″ long and two 1″ long. Position these supports at either side of stairs, with shorter supports at the end of the stairs, longer supports flush with front edge of top stair. Make pilot holes with skewer, add glue, then press supports ¼″ into plastic foam base. Cut handrails to span the distance from the short railing supports to the columns flanking the doorway. Glue these in place.

SUMMER CENTERPIECE
continued

Landscaping: For a lawn, cover the base around the gazebo with glue. Cover glue with sawdust and let dry. When glue is dry, mix equal parts Clover paint, Emerald Green paint, and water. Paint this mixture over the sawdust; any excess sawdust will be removed during this process.

Mix a brown wash as before. Brush on any parts of the wooden structure that seem too white, over any visible glue, and over any patchy parts of green base. Let dry. Glue steps in place.

For woodland ferns, poke a few holes around bottom of platform, fill with glue, and set small pieces of Plumosis. For a wisteria vine, cut a 20″ length of twisted paper for the main vine. Guide the main vine from the base, up to the roof and around the roof, under the twig "eaves," securing it along the way with floral wire wrapped to columns, piercing the foam of the base or the foam of the roof. Also use floral wire to wrap and secure pieces of Ming Fern along this main vine, and also spiraling up the roof. Make wisteria flower clusters as follows: Thread 1 strand of embroidery floss onto a beading needle, and knot the thread 3″ from the end. Then thread 5 larger (antique or glass) beads onto thread. Add 6 petite glass beads, then run the needle through the first larger bead. Thread 6 more petite seed beads on to the thread, then run the needle through the last larger bead, thread 6 onto thread, run needle through first larger bead. Tie the ends in a secure knot. Make 7 flower clusters in this way, then make 7 more in the same way, but having 5 groups of petite seed beads. Tie flower clusters along vine so they hang down; trim thread ends.

Finishing: Place base on felt, and trace around. Cut out felt, and glue to the underside of the base. Glue a charm securely to tip of roof, for a decoration or weathervane. Glue butterflies over the centerpiece at random or as desired. ◊

WINTER CENTERPIECE: SNOWBALL HOUSE

Dimensions: House, about 3″ high; base, 9″ x 5″

Materials & Tools

- *Styrofoam brand plastic foam: egg, 3¹³/₁₆″ x 2¹³/₁₆″, block, 12″ x 12″ x ½″ thick*
- *Aleene's Thick Designer Tacky *Glue*
- *Forster Wooden Products: 4 small and 1 medium pieces woodsy squares; 1 craft stick*
- *Toothpicks*
- *Small twigs for bare trees, snowman arms, porch uprights*
- *Small pod or nutshell, for porch roof*
- *Wel-Cote Dry Powder Spackling Rapid-Bond 45*
- *3-4 large pine cones, for roof shingles, plus 3 mini pine cones, for shrubs*
- *Gold bead, 5mm, for doorknob*
- *3 small white pom-poms: one ³/₈″; one ½″; one ⁵/₈″*
- *White sewing thread*
- *Ultra-fine "Crystal Snow," #GM900U, from Mark Enterprises*
- *Acrylic paint: 2 oz. white pearl; small amounts of red, brown and orange*

- *1 flat river stone, plus a few pieces of gravel*
- *1 package Setaria, dyed Hunter Green—item 6942-50*
- *1 package Illusion Galaxy (bleached gyp dusted with fine glitter)*
- *Kunin Felt; 9″ x 12″ sheet in white*
- *Utility knife*
- *Spatula*
- *Clippers*
- *Sanford "Sharpie" extra fine point permanent markers in black and brown*
- *Sewing needle*
- *Paintbrushes*
- *Container for mixing spackling compound*
- *Mini glue gun and hot-melt glue sticks*

Directions

Construction: Cut about 1″ from the wider end of the plastic foam egg. From the plastic foam block, cut an irregular circle, 9″ in diameter, then trim it to form a 9″ x 5″ kidney-shaped base. Use tacky glue to adhere the cut-off section to the narrow end of the base, for a hill. Glue the flat side of the egg to the center of the wide end, for the house.

Applying Stucco and Snow: Mix spackling compound according to the manufacturer's instructions. Use a spatula to spread this mixture smoothly over all surfaces of the egg—except for the bottom of the base. It should be less smooth over the base, including the hill. Create snow swirls and drifts, and scrape a pathway from what will be the front of the house to the front of the base. Let dry.

Making the House: For the roof, use clippers to remove the stem plus about 3 rows of petals from one large pine cone, and the petals from another couple of pine cones. Hot-glue single petals around the egg—about 2″ above the base. Overlap rounds of petals, then hot-glue the stem end on top. For the door, use a utility knife to cut a medium wooden square in half for a base, and to cut craft sticks lengthwise and crosswise to form the arch shown in the actual size pattern, below. Use tacky glue to adhere the craft stick pieces to the base. Paint the door red, then glue the base to the house so that the pathway ends at the door. Hot-glue a gold bead to the door, for a doorknob. Hot-glue a river stone, for a doorstep. Use a skewer to poke a small hole on either side of the doorstep. Adding a bit of glue, insert a 1³⁄₄″ long twig that forks at the top into each hole, for porch supports. Hot-glue a pod or nutshell over the porch supports.

For windows, use 2 small wooden squares. Use brown marker to outline each square and draw horizontal and vertical lines to divide the windows into panes. For shutters, cut 2 small wooden squares in half. Paint red, then draw stripes across them with brown marker. Hot-glue shutters over ends of each window, then hot-glue windows on either side of door.

Landscaping: First, make the snowman: sew pom-poms together in a graduated row, keeping the thread ends long. Hang the pom-poms by this thread, and cover them with spackling compound. Let dry completely, then glue to the base as shown in the photograph.

Apply white pearl paint over all the snowy areas, including the snowman. Except for the tips of the roof shingles, do not paint the house. While the paint is still wet, sprinkle it with crystal snow. With permanent marker, make "coal" for eyes, smile, and buttons on snowman. Pierce the head with the tip of a toothpick, painted orange, for a "carrot" nose. Also use a toothpick to pierce holes on either side of the midsection, and insert short twigs, for arms. Hot-glue the calyx from a dried pod on top, for a hat.

To set "trees" and "shrubs" into the base, first poke holes in the snow with a toothpick. Fill the hole with glue. Clip stems very short on dried florals, then insert stems into holes. Surround the house with Setaria "evergreens," mini pine cone "shrubs," twig trees, and then with many sprigs of Illusion Galaxy. Lightly brush edges of evergreens and shrubs with white pearl paint, and sprinkle with crystal snow. Apply glue along the pathway, and set in pieces of gravel.

Finishing: Place the base on felt and trace around it. Cut out the felt, and glue it to the underside of the base.

Actual-Size Pattern for Door

Embroidery Stitch Details

Couching

French knot

Lazy Daisy Stitch

Running Stitch

Straight Stitch

Additional Ribbonwork Techniques

Loop Stitch

Folded Rose

Japanese Ribbon Stitch

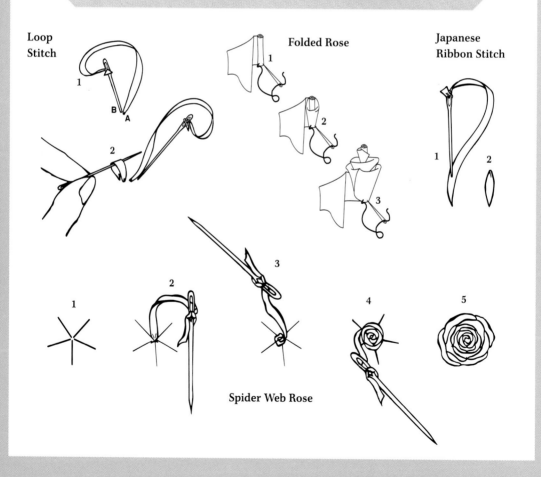

Spider Web Rose

How to Cross Stitch

New, unwashed even-weave fabrics have a crispness that makes a hoop helpful but not necessary. The 6-strand rayon floss specified in this book is color-fast, and the 6-strand metallic embroidery floss is resistant to tarnish. Iron the fabric first. Cut out a fabric piece, leaving at least 2" more all around than the dimensions of finished piece (more if you will use a hoop). Stitch or tape the edges of the fabric to prevent fraying. To locate the center of the fabric, fold it in quarters; mark the center with a pin and unfold. To locate the center of the chart, follow the arrows; mark the center with a colored pencil. Begin at the center of the chart and the fabric, and work to one side, then to the other. If arrows point to a blank area, count squares to the nearest symbol, then count threads to arrive at the corresponding intersection of threads on the fabric.

For most projects in this book, each symbol on a chart represents 1 cross stitch worked over 2-by-2 threads of the fabric. Refer to the key for colors. Separate the strands of floss and thread the number of strands in needle as indicated in the individual directions. For rayon and metallic floss, work with strands no more than 12" long, to prevent tangling or fraying. To begin stitching, leave a tail on the back and stitch over it to anchor it. To end, run the needle under 4 or 5 stitches on the back; do not make knots. Work each area of color individually.

For a single cross stitch, use 2 motions. Referring to figure 1, bring the threaded needle up at 1, down at 2, up at 3, and down at 4, completing the stitch. Make crosses touch by inserting the needle in the same hole used for the adjacent stitch. Work horizontal rows of stitches whenever possible. Referring to figure 2, bring the thread up at 1 and down at 2, repeat this diagonal stitch to the end of the row of the same color, forming the first half of each stitch. Complete the stitches by stitching diagonally in the opposite direction; refer to the 3-4 movement in figure 3. When it makes sense to work vertically, complete each stitch, then proceed to the next. In any case, make sure that all stitches appear uniform: that all underneath stitches slant in one and the same direction, and that all top stitches slant in the opposite direction.

Various short diagonal lines on the chart are half cross stitches. Pay attention to the direction of these lines. Often a short or long line represents backstitches. Follow the numbers and arrows on figure 4; the backstitch is in red. Refer to the key for colors, and work each backstitch over 2 threads of the fabric, unless otherwise indicated. Incorporate these stitches into your cross stitching to avoid extra color changes.

Lightly iron the finished cross stitch, using a press cloth (especially with metallic threads!) and steam. If there are beads on your piece, place the piece right side down over a padded surface, and iron from the back.

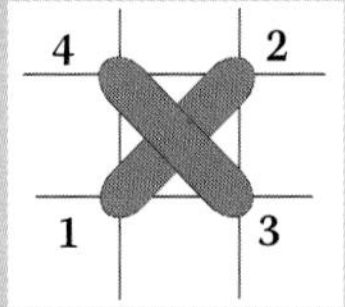

Figure 1

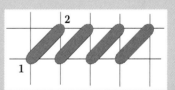

Figure 2

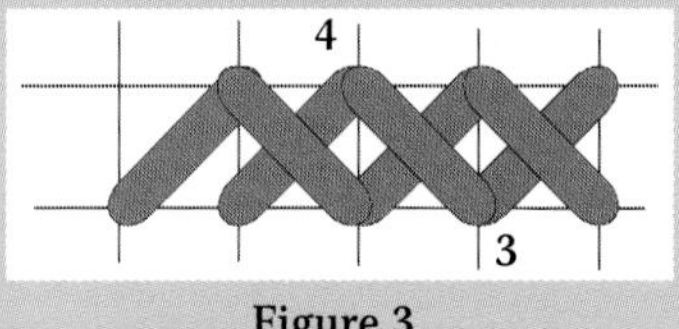

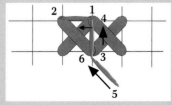

Figure 3

Figure 4

Sources

Unless otherwise indicated, check your local crafts and sewing stores for the products used in this book. For more information, contact the companies listed here.

Aleene's/Artis Inc.
85 Industrial Way
Buellton, CA 93427
800–825–3363
Glue, shrink–art plastic

American Art Clay Co., Inc.
4717 W. 16th St.
Indianapolis, IN 46222
317–244–6871
fax: 317–248–9300
e–mail: amacobrent@aol.com
www.iquest.net/amaco/
Fimo, Friendly Plastic, Rub 'n Buff, molds, tools

American Traditional Stencils
442 1st New Hampshire
    Turnpike
Northwood, NH 03261
800-448-6656
fax: 800-448-6654
Stencils and supplies

Anne Brinkley Designs
12 Chestnut Hill Lane
Lincroft, NJ 07758
908-530-5432
Brooch frames

Beadworks
149 Water St.
South Norwalk, CT 06854
203-852-9108
fax: 203-855-8015
Beads

Bucilla Ribbons
Bucilla Corporation
1 Oak Ridge Road
Hazelton, PA 18201
800-233-3239
fax: 800-453-3316
Silk embroidery ribbons

The Caron Collection
55 Old South Ave.
Stratford, CT 06497
203-381-9999
Silk and wool threads

Coats & Clark
Consumer Service
P.O. Box 12229
Greenville, SC 29612-0229
e-mail: www.coatsandclark
    .com
Anchor floss, sewing thread

Creative Beginnings
475 Morro Bay Blvd.
Morro Bay, CA 93442
800-367-1739
fax: 805-772-5845
Charms

The DMC Corporation
10 Port Kearny
South Kearny, NJ 07032-4688
201-589-0606
fax: 201-589-8931
www.dmc-usa.com
Six–strand embroidery floss, rayon floss, 6–strand metallic floss, embroidery thread, tatting thread

Darice
21160 Drake Rd.
Strongville, OH 44136
216-238-9150
Plastic canvas

DecoArt
Hwy. Junction 150 & 27
Stanford, KY 40484
606-365-3193
Americana acrylic paints

Dress It Up (a Jesse James Company)
615 North New Street
Allentown, PA 18102
610-435-7899
fax: 610435-8149
e-mail: eatkins100@aol.com
www.amsn.com/jessejames
Assortments of embellishments for crafts

Environmental Technologies, Inc.
P.O. Box 365
Fields Landing, CA 95537-
    0365
800-368-9323
EnviroTex Lite

Fiskars Inc.
7811 West Stewart Ave.
Wausau, WI 54401
715-842-2091
fax: 715-848-3657
Paper edgers

Forster Inc.
P.O. Box 657
Wilton, ME 04294-0657
207-897-4229
fax:207-645-9317
Craft sticks and wood pieces

Handler Textile Corp.
Consumer Products Division
24 Empire Blvd.
Moonachie, NJ 07074
800-666-0335
*Interfacings and patchwork
foundations*

Kreinik Manufacturing Co.
3106 Timanus Lane, Suite 101
Baltimore, MD 21244
410-281-0040
fax: 410-281-2519
Fancy threads

Kunin Felt
380 Lafayette Rd.
Hampton, NH 03842
603-929-6100
Kreative Kanvas, felt

Lion Ribbons
C.M. Offray & Son, Inc.
Route 24/ Box 601
Chester, NJ07930
908-879-4700
fax: 908-879-8588
Ribbons

Mark Enterprises
873 West 15th St., Unit C
Newport Beach, CA 92663
717-631-9200
fax: 714-631-1244
Crystal Snow

Mill Hill
P.O. Box 1060
Janesville, WI 53547-1060
800-447-1332
fax: 608-754-0665
http://www.millhill.com
*Mill Hill Glass Beads,
Framecraft boxes and jewelry
settings, perforated paper*

Mokuba Ribbon
561 Seventh Ave.
New York, New York 10018
888-466-5822
fax: 212-221-6676
Ribbons

Panacea Products Corp.
1825 Joyce Ave.
Columbus, OH 43219
614-272-0282
fax: 614-276-9807
Floral supplies

Plaid Enterprises, Inc.
1649 International Ct.
Norcross, GA 30091-7600
770-923-8200
fax: 770-381-3404
www:plaidonline.com
*FolkArt and Apple Barrel
acrylic paints*

Polyform Products Co.
1901 Estes Ave.
Elk Grove Village, IL 60007
847-427-0020
fax: 847-427-0426
*Sculpey III, Granitex polymer
clays*

Royal China & Porcelain
Available at specialty retail
stores; for further information contact
800-257-7189
Demitasses

Rubber Stampede
P.O. Box 246
Berkeley, CA 94701
800-632-8386
Rubber stamps and supplies

Styrofoam
The Dow Chemical Co.
Inquiry and Distribution
Services
P.O. Box 1206
Midland, MI 46874
Styrofoam brand plastic foam

Sulky of America
3113 Broadpoint Dr.
Harbor Heights, FL 33983
800-874-4115
941-629-3199
fax: 941-743-4634
*Specialty threads for sewing
machines*

Viking Husqvarna & White
11760 Berea Rd.
Cleveland, OH 44111
216-252-3300
fax: 216-252-3311
*Sewing machines, The Spinster
and other sewing accessories*

Westrim Crafts
9667 Canoga Ave.
Chatsworth, CA 91311
800-727-2727
fax: 818-709-9028
*Trimmings, miniature accesso-
ries, miscellaneous craft
supplies*

Zweigart
Needleworker's Delight
Mail Order Co.
100 Claridge Place
Colonia, NJ 07067
800-931-4545 or
908-388-4545
Even–weave fabrics

Acknowledgments

The subject matter is miniature, but the work on this book was grand scale, and I owe a huge debt of gratitude to many big-hearted people who helped me. First and foremost, I thank the creative goddesses. All of the professional designers I called upon are major talents with tremendous flair for small-scale, do-able projects. They followed me into unmapped territory and delivered the goods far beyond my wildest dreams. On board from nearly the start, my art director, Lisa Palmer, provided this book with its classic good looks. Without exception, she demonstrated unlimited versatility, patience, and good humor.

Great designs deserve great photography. George Ross, master of light and film, always romanced each shot as if it were the only one that counted. Assisting George on location, Lewis Bloom tirelessly oversaw every detail and caught my oversights, no matter how late the hour. A novice but none-the-less professional, Tracey Hanover worked independently, yet still endowed all of the close-up shots with grace and clarity. She even makes me look good in the photograph below! Iris Richardson graciously shared her studio, her props, and her ideas with Tracey.

I am indebted to Seiche Sanders and Don Gulbrandsen, at Krause, for their support, trust, and expertise. Jane "Shana" Blum charted in a way that only a true needleworker can appreciate. Eric Merrill, a computer graphics magician, imported Jane's charts and transformed all of my very rough sketches into technical illustrations par excellence—in next to no time.

In the crafts and miniatures industry, there were many who answered my calls for help. Certain publicity directors and their bosses who manufacture the craft products used prominently in this book served as my "patrons of the arts." Bucilla supplied the lovely stitch details on page 124. Susan Brandt and Judy O'Brien at the Hobby Industry Association (HIA), and Debbie Johnston at the Miniatures Industry Association (MIA) tracked down resources.

Friends and family are last but never least on a list like this. Good buddy Bonita Salamanca checked and styled all the crochet directions. She let me rifle through her knickknacks and dollhouses as I looked for props, and she scouted out the perfect pieces for me elsewhere. That included the little doll bed and Victorian crib from the "Sign of the Black Duck," a lovely dollhouse and miniatures store Jean Karsan runs in Stockton, New Jersey. Janice Nawn lent me her family pictures and her creative insights. Hiroko Kiiffner encouraged me to finally join her ranks as a book packager and navigated the circuitous paths of legal contracts for me. My wonderful husband eased my endless anxieties and edited my introductory text. Despite the tiny scale of the projects, my work in designing, photostyling, researching, and writing this book completely overran our home and our home life, and my family accepted that with their usual aplomb. ◊

About the Author

Eleanor Levie has been an author and editor for dozens of books and magazines in needlework and crafts. Ms. Levie is the author of *Great Little Quilts, Country Living Handmade Country, Country Living Country Paint,* and *Halloween Fun.* She was an editor at *McCall's Needlework & Crafts, Woman's World,* and *First,* and produced special interest crafts and do-it-yourself decorating magazines for *Woman's Day* and *Country Accents.* She teaches crafts in workshops for adults and children.

Ms. Levie initiated all of the projects for *Creations in Miniature,* most of which were then developed and created by the highly talented designers named throughout this book. As a queen of the quick-and-easy, Ms. Levie enjoyed adding her own designs to the mix.

When not at her home computer, sewing machine, or craft table, Ms. Levie volunteers as an advocate for women's and children's issues, and is an organizer of social action projects in her community. She lives in Bucks County, Pennsylvania, with her husband, Carl Harrington, and their son, Sam. ◊